The CP/M Plus
Handbook

The CP/M Plus™
Handbook

Alan R. Miller

Berkeley · Paris · Düsseldorf

Cover art by Nicolae Razumieff
Book design by Sharon Leong
Cartoons by Gar Smith

BADLIM is a trademark of Blat Research & Development Corporation.
CP/M is a registered trademark of Digital Research, Inc.
CP/M Plus is a trademark of Digital Research, Inc.
FILEFIX © 1983, Alan Miller.
Grammatik is a trademark of Aspen Software Co.
Intel is a registered trademark of Intel Corporation.
MAC is a trademark of Digital Research, Inc.
MACRO-80 is a trademark of Microsoft Corporation.
MBASIC is a trademark of Microsoft Corporation.
NorthStar Horizon is a trademark of Northstar Computers, Inc.
RMAC is a trademark of Digital Research, Inc.
SID is a trademark of Digital Research, Inc.
Spellguard is a trademark of Sorcim Corporation.
SuperSort is a trademark of MicroPro International Corporation.
WordStar is a trademark of MicroPro International Corporation.
Z80 is a registered trademark of Zilog, Inc.

SYBEX is not affiliated with any manufacturer.

Every effort has been made to supply complete and accurate information. However, SYBEX assumes
no responsibility for its use, nor for any infringements of patents or other rights of third parties which
would result.

Library of Congress Card Number: 84-50033
ISBN 0-89588-158-6
Printed in the United States of America
10 9 8 7 6 5 4 3 2 1

Contents

PREFACE   x

1 **Getting Started**   **1**

Introduction   1
What Is a Microcomputer?   2
The Hardware   2
The Software   5
Floppy Disks   6
Starting Up and Turning Off the Computer   12
Summary   14

2 **Learning to Use CP/M Plus**   **17**

Introduction   17
What Is CP/M Plus?   18

Trying Out CP/M   19
Control Characters   23
Duplicating Disks   27
Some Elementary Operations with PIP   33
Displaying and Printing a File   36
Files and File Names   38
Summary   44

3 Commonly Used Commands   47

Introduction   47
Commands and Parameters   48
Built-in Commands and Transient Programs   51
Five Important Transient Programs   65
Summary   84

4 Handling Files with PIP   87

Introduction   87
Copying Files   89
Concatenating Files   100
Transferring a Disk File
to a Peripheral Device   104
Setting Up a New User Area   111
Copying Read-Only and System Files   113
Zeroing the Parity Bit   114
Using Option Parameters with PIP   115
Summary   116

5 *The System Editor, ED*   **119**

Introduction   119
What Is a Text Editor?   120
How ED Operates   121
Using ED   124
Commands for Manipulating
the Character Pointer   128
Commands for Altering Text
in the Edit Buffer   135
Moving a Block of Text   138
Repeating Groups of Commands   139
Completing the Editing Session   141
Summary   144

6 *Inside CP/M Plus*   **147**

Introduction   147
The Components of CP/M Plus   148
The Organization of CP/M Plus   150
The Operation of CP/M Plus   153
Summary   162

7 *A Quick Reference to
CP/M Commands and Programs*   **165**

Introduction   165
COPY, COPYSYS, DATE, DEVICE, DIR, DIRSYS,
DUMP, ED, ERASE, FORMAT, GENCOM, GET,
HELP, HEXCOM, INITDIR, LIB, LINK, MAC,

PATCH, PIP, PUT, RENAME, RMAC, SAVE, SET,
SETDEF, SHOW, SID, SUBMIT, TYPE, USER, XREF

Appendices

A   CP/M Plus and CP/M Version 2
    Compared   225
B   Practical Hints   231
C   The CP/M Control Characters   241
D   ASCII Character Set   243

INDEX   244

Preface

The purpose ot this book is to teach you how to use the CP/M Plus™ operating system. You do not need any prior knowledge of computer operation. However, if you already know something about CP/M®, you can use this book to learn more. You can also use the book as a reference work since all the CP/M commands are summarized in Chapter 7.

CP/M is the most common microcomputer operating system. Digital Research has steadily improved the system from its introduction as version 1.3. The latest version, 3.0, is so different from earlier ones that Digital Research has added the word Plus to the name.

I have used CP/M from its beginning, starting with version 1.3. During this time I installed CP/M on several different computers, including the original Altair 8800 and a North Star Horizon™. For more information on the internal workings of CP/M and how to add useful features, see my *Mastering CP/M* (SYBEX, 1983).

This book is designed to be read from the beginning, especially by those who have just acquired a CP/M computer, though more experienced readers can use it for reference. For those who are using a computer for the first time, Chapter 1 is a brief introduction to the components and operations of microcomputers. If you feel comfortable working with a microcomputer and are ready to start learning about CP/M Plus, you can skip this chapter.

Chapter 2 introduces you to the CP/M Plus operating system and some of its basic functions. Numerous examples will enable you to enter simple commands and edit them; format and duplicate disks; and create, display, and print a file. By the end of the chapter you should have a feeling for one of CP/M's most useful programs, PIP, as well as for the various control characters you will use frequently.

Chapter 3 explains in some detail the six built-in commands of CP/M Plus—TYPE, USER, DIR, DIRSYS, RENAME, and ERASE. It also discusses five transient programs—SETDEF, SHOW, SET, SUBMIT, and DEVICE.

Chapter 4 is entirely devoted to PIP, a program for duplicating and altering computer programs. Chapter 5 shows how to use the CP/M editor, ED, for creating and altering your own computer programs and textual material.

The first five chapters give you all the information you need to use CP/M Plus effectively. If you want to know more about how the system works, Chapter 6 provides a detailed discussion of the inner workings of CP/M Plus.

The first six chapters are a tutorial on the operation of CP/M Plus. By contrast, Chapter 7 summarizes all the CP/M commands and programs in alphabetical order. Thus, it provides a quick reference when you need details about a particular operation.

Four appendices present additional reference material. Appendix A compares CP/M Plus with the previous version, CP/M 2.2. Appendix B is a collection of practical hints for using and caring for your computer, and hints for using the operations most effectively. Appendix C lists and explains the CP/M control characters, and Appendix D is a table of the ASCII character set.

The manuscript for this book was created and edited with WordStar™ running on a Z80® computer. The spelling was checked with

Spellguard™ and the syntax was checked with Grammatik™. The final manuscript was submitted to SYBEX on a magnetic disk compatible with the photocomposer. I am sincerely grateful to Susan Weisberg, editor of the manuscript, for all her helpful suggestions, and to Joel Kreisman for technical review.

Alan R. Miller
Socorro, New Mexico
September 1983

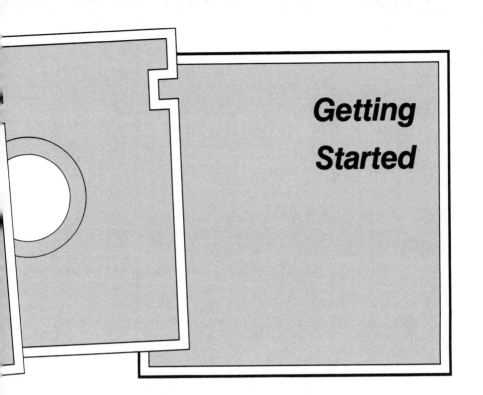

Getting Started

INTRODUCTION

This chapter introduces you to the operation of a microcomputer. You do not need any previous experience with computers to understand it. We will define the essential terminology and describe the basic procedures.

If you have used a microcomputer before and are familiar with the various components and operations, you can skip this chapter and begin with Chapter 2. If you're new to computers, this chapter will give you enough information to begin working with the CP/M Plus operating system. You can find more about the workings and use of microcomputers in two other books published by SYBEX: *Your First Computer,* new updated edition, and *Don't! (or How to Care for Your Computer),* both by Rodnay Zaks.

WHAT IS A MICROCOMPUTER?

The purpose of a computer is to manipulate information, whether it is a NASA computer calculating the path of a rocket or a personal computer organizing a mailing list. This book will deal with the operation of microcomputers—small, self-sufficient computers.

A computer actually has two elements that work together. The *hardware* comprises the physical parts of the computer: the central processing unit, main memory, video screen, keyboard, disks and disk drives, printer, and any additional parts. The *software* is the intangible aspect of the computer—the programs and data that make it work. A computer needs both hardware and software to run.

THE HARDWARE

Computer hardware may be combined in various ways. Figure 1.1, for example, shows a computer with three separate parts: the CRT terminal with its video screen; a housing containing the central processing unit (CPU), the main memory, and the disk drives; and the keyboard. In the portable computer in Figure 1.2, the video screen is contained in the same housing as the CPU, the main memory, and the disks. The separate keyboard is attached by a plug-in cord. Additional hardware, such as a modem or a tape recorder, may also be attached to a computer system. These additional elements are sometimes called *peripherals.*

Let's take a brief look at each component.

The Main Computer Unit

The hardware element that directs all the computer's operations is the *central processing unit,* or CPU. For microcomputers this is a

Figure 1.1 – *A Microcomputer with Three Separate Components*

Figure 1.2 – *A Portable Microcomputer*

single integrated circuit, etched on a silicon chip. The operation of the CPU is controlled by programs stored in the computer's *main memory.*

The purpose of the computer's memory is to store information, either programs or data you enter for processing. The memory size is measured in bytes or kilobytes. A *byte* represents a single character, such as the letter B. A *kilobyte,* usually abbreviated as K, is approximately 1,000 bytes. Typical microcomputer memory sizes are 16K, 32K, 48K, 64K, and 128K bytes. The computer's memory is often called the *RAM,* which stands for random access memory.

The Console
(Video Display and Keyboard)

The *console* consists of a video screen or televisionlike terminal and a keyboard. It is the primary means by which the user interacts with the computer. You enter information by typing on the keyboard, and the computer places your information into its memory. The computer uses the video screen to display both your entries and the results of its computations. A video screen that is physically separate from the keyboard is called a *monitor.*

The advantage of a video screen is that it can display information very rapidly. The disadvantage is that there is no permanent record of the information. When new information appears on the video screen, the previously displayed information is lost. For this reason computers can include a printer so that you can have a permanent record.

The Printer

The printer provides a permanent printout of information, known as a *hard copy.* The information can be the result of computations, the listing of a program, or simply a record of information that the user entered at the keyboard.

The Disks and Disk Drives

With the present technology, most of the computer's memory is volatile. That is, the information it contains is lost each time the computer is turned off. In addition, the memory is limited in size. Consequently, the programs and data must be stored on some permanent medium. When the computer needs to use the stored information, it *loads* the information into the main memory. This doesn't mean the information is actually removed from permanent storage. In effect, the computer just memorizes it temporarily. The original version also remains in storage.

Microcomputers use magnetic disks or tapes for storage. As CP/M Plus is a disk-based operating system, we will discuss only disk storage in this book.

There are two kinds of *disks*—flexible, or floppy, disks and rigid, or hard, disks. The capacity of a disk is given in kilobytes or megabytes (a little more than a million bytes). We will describe floppy disks in detail after we discuss software.

Each *disk drive* contains a drive motor to rotate the disk, a read/write head, and a motor to position the head. The computer readily encodes and retrieves information on the disk surface through the read/write head.

THE SOFTWARE

A computer needs a set of instructions, called a program, to make it perform properly. Once installed in the computer's memory, the program will direct the computer to perform specific operations. Computer programs, as well as any data needed to run a program, are called *software*.

Software can be divided into two basic categories—system software and applications software. The *system software* is a collection of programs that the computer requires in order to operate. Most of the necessary system programs are provided with the computer when you buy it. It is also possible to purchase additional system software. The CP/M Plus operating system, which includes such "housekeeping" programs as PIP and ED, is part of your system software.

Applications software is the collection of programs you use to perform specific tasks. For example, a word processor such as WordStar, a spreadsheet program such as SuperCalc™, a mailing list program, an inventory program, a general ledger program, and a data-base manager are common applications software. We will devote little of this book to applications programs since there are separate books and manuals for this purpose.

Data are collections of characters or numbers—for example, the names and addresses to go on a mailing list—that are manipulated by programs. Data and programs are stored on a disk in logical groupings known as *files,* to which the user assigns unique names for easy reference. Later in this book you will learn how to create and manipulate files and how to use a variety of programs.

An *operating system* is a computer program that manages the resources of the computer. The operating system reads commands from the keyboard, displays information on the video screen and printer, and executes applications programs for the user. In addition, the operating system will perform internal chores, such as managing the disk space and the main memory space of the computer. CP/M Plus is the latest version of the most common microcomputer operating system.

FLOPPY DISKS

As we mentioned earlier, microcomputers use magnetic disks to store information. The most common type is the *floppy disk,* also called simply a disk or floppy. Disks are available in several formats. The two most common types of floppy disk—8-inch diameter and 5¼-inch diameter (called simply 5-inch in this book)—are illustrated in Figures 1.3 and 1.4.

This section will describe how floppy disks work and explain how to use them. Further hints for using disks are included in Appendix B, "Practical Hints."

Physical Details of the Disk

A disk is made of mylar coated with a magnetic oxide material. A

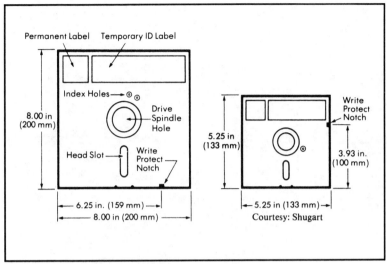

Figure 1.3 – Floppy Disks

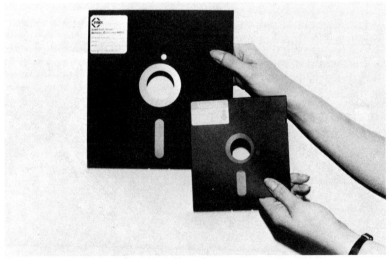

Figure 1.4 – 5-Inch and 8-Inch Floppy Disks Compared

square outer envelope lined with a soft material protects the flexible disk within. When the disk is in use, it rotates at high speed inside its envelope. The central hole allows the disk drive motor to rotate the disk. The slot or long opening in the envelope (shown in Figure 1.5) allows the read/write head to contact the disk surface and to read or

Figure 1.5 – The Slot Allows the Read/Write Head to Contact the Disk.

write information on it the way sound is recorded on magnetic tape. The rotating disk interrupts a light beam projected through the index hole. In this way the computer can determine the exact position of the disk.

Information is recorded on the disk surface along concentric circles called *tracks,* which are partitioned into smaller regions known as *sectors* (see Figure 1.6). Disks are made in two ways, known as hard sectored and soft sectored. In addition, they may be single or double sided and single or double density. You do not need to understand the technical details of disks in order to use them. However, it is important to use the correct type, so be sure to buy disks like the one that came with your computer.

Write-Protection

Disks are often—but not always—equipped with a *write-protect* notch (see Figure 1.7). With a standard 8-inch disk the notch may be omitted or it may be covered by a piece of aluminum tape. If this tape

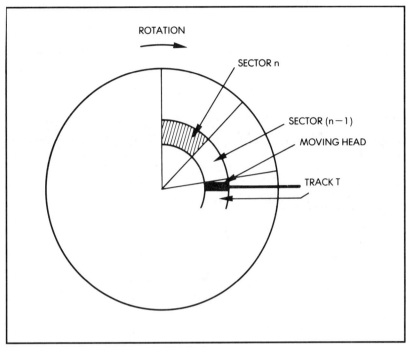

Figure 1.6 – *Tracks and Sectors of a Disk Surface*

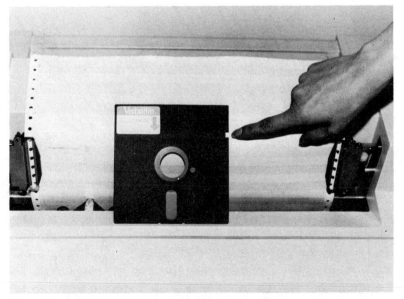

Figure 1.7 – *A 5-inch Disk with Write-Protect Notch Uncovered*

is removed, the notch is exposed and the disk drive is no longer able to record, or write, on the disk.

The opposite is true with 5-inch disks. The aluminum tape must be removed in order to write on the disk. When the tape is positioned over the notch, the disk can only be read.

Write-protection is used to protect important information. For example, master disks, which are not used regularly, are normally write protected.

Handling Disks

Floppy disks are delicate and can be easily damaged. Always treat disks with care. You can grasp a disk by its outer envelope, but do not touch the exposed magnetic surface areas. Be sure not to expose the disk to dust, smoke, or liquids. It is very important to keep the disk away from magnetic fields or metal that can be magnetized. Do not write on the disk envelope with a ball pen or a pencil as the impression of the writing instrument can damage the underlying surface. Mark the disk only with a felt-tipped pen or write on a separate label and then affix the label to the disk. Read Appendix B for more hints on handling disks. You can also use that appendix for reminders when you are more experienced.

The Disk Drive

It is important to insert disks into your computer correctly. In general, the "rule of thumb" applies—hold the disk with your thumb on the label as you insert it into the drive (see Figure 1.8). If the disk drive has a door, the label usually faces the door handle. If you are practicing for the first time, use a brand new disk rather a disk with important information on it.

A disk should never be removed from or inserted into a disk drive when the computer is reading or writing on that drive. Furthermore,

Figure 1.8 – Inserting a Disk into the Computer

never shut off your computer when it is reading or writing a disk. A red light on the front of the drive usually indicates the disk is being read or written by the computer. To be safe, always check to be sure that the light is off before removing or inserting a disk.

It is good practice to remove all floppy disks before turning off the computer even though it is not necessary for some brands of computers.

Now that you have learned some of the basic concepts and how to handle floppy disks, it is time to begin using the computer.

STARTING UP AND TURNING OFF THE COMPUTER

To begin, turn on your computer and the peripherals and insert the system disk in the drive according to the manufacturer's directions. In order for the computer to function, the operating system must be loaded into the main memory by a special program called a *bootstrap loader*. Each time the computer is turned on either the bootstrap loader automatically loads CP/M Plus into the memory, or you give a specific command that loads it, depending on which computer you have. This is known as a *cold start,* or *booting* the system.

Once CP/M Plus is loaded, the operating system takes control and waits for you to type a command. Try typing something such as:

HELLO THERE

Then press the key marked RETURN or ENTER. The screen will show what you typed followed by a question mark, since it is not pro-grammed for this command. The computer will then wait for your next request. You cannot hurt the hardware by typing at the terminal. You might, however, alter one of the programs stored on disk if you keep typing without knowing what you are doing. Now it is time to turn off the computer so you can go on the Chapter 2, where you will begin learning the CP/M Plus operating system.

You do not turn off your automobile engine while waiting for a red light to turn green. In the same way, it is a good idea not to turn off your computer each time you have finished a task. Rather, it is usually best to turn on your computer at the beginning of the day and turn it off at the end of the day. If you expect electrical interruptions because of lightning, for example, then it is best to turn the computer off when it is not in use.

When you are ready to turn off your computer, make sure that the computer is not reading or writing a disk. Remove all floppy disks, place them into their envelopes, and put them away in a box. Then turn off the computer according to the manufacturer's directions.

SUMMARY

This chapter introduced you to microcomputers. We described the basic hardware elements: the central processing unit, the console, the printer, and the disks and disk drive. We briefly explained the software and operating system the computer uses to perform its functions. The section on floppy disks described disks and gave some hints for using them. Finally, we explained turning the computer on and off. You have mastered the fundamentals of microcomputers. You're now ready to begin learning CP/M Plus.

Learning to Use CP/M Plus

INTRODUCTION

Now that you know the do's and don'ts of using a microcomputer, you can begin to learn how to use the CP/M Plus operating system. This chapter will introduce you to some of the basic features and commands of CP/M, many of which we will explore in detail in later chapters. By the end of this chapter, you will be familiar enough with CP/M to be able to run most applications programs on your computer.

WHAT IS CP/M PLUS?

An operating system is a program that manages the resources of the computer. The operating system reads commands from the keyboard, displays information on the video screen and printer, and runs applications programs for the user. In addition, the operating system performs internal chores, such as managing the disk space and the main memory space of the computer.

Each computer system has its own set of hardware combined in particular ways. To run on a given computer, an applications program must be able to interact with that system. With so many different types of computers available, it would be impractical to design a separate version of each program to fit each system. This problem is solved by having an operating system that can run on many types of computer and then tailoring the program to that operating system.

It is important to know what operating system your computer uses. A program written for CP/M Plus cannot be expected to work on a different operating system.

CP/M Plus (also known as CP/M version 3) is the latest version of CP/M (an acronym for Control Program for Microprocessors), the most common microcomputer operating system. CP/M Plus contains several very useful new features in addition to many that are the same as in earlier versions of CP/M. For simplicity, in this book we will refer to the system as CP/M and draw attention to features available only with version 3. If you have used earlier versions of CP/M, you may find it helpful to read Appendix A, which summarizes the new features and compares CP/M Plus with earlier versions. For detailed explanation of earlier versions, see *The CP/M Handbook,* by Rodnay Zaks (SYBEX, 1980).

We should note that CP/M Plus is available in two forms, known as banked and nonbanked. It is not necessary for you to understand the technical details of these forms, though they are explained in Chapter 6 and Appendix A, if you are interested. The nonbanked form is intended primarily for programmers or for older machines with insufficient memory for the banked version. Consequently, it is likely you are running a banked form. Therefore, this book discusses all the features for the banked form with a note included whenever a particular feature is not available to the nonbanked form.

How CP/M Works

CP/M is a collection of programs on your system disk. Each time you turn on your computer, CP/M must be loaded into the main memory, as explained in Chapter 1. Once installed in the memory, CP/M becomes an integral part of the computer and starts monitoring the keyboard for commands. At this point, you can enter into a dialogue with CP/M and activate the applications program you want to use.

You can view CP/M as a servant always ready to obey your commands as long as you are not running an applications program. In that case, all your dialogue is with the applications program. When the applications program finishes, CP/M is activated again and is ready to accept new commands.

In the following sections we will try out CP/M and begin learning the basic commands.

TRYING OUT CP/M

Turn on your computer. If you have an automatic bootstrap loader, it will copy CP/M into memory after you place the system disk into disk drive A. Otherwise, you must enter a special command at the keyboard directing the monitor to load CP/M. Sometimes you will have to begin by entering the current date (or return).

Symbols on the Screen

When CP/M has been successfully loaded, the video screen displays:

A>

The A> is a *prompt,* a message or symbol that CP/M displays to indicate that it is ready to accept your next command. In this case, the
letter also indicates the *default* disk drive, the drive you are currently
working on. If your computer only has one disk drive, it will be called
A. If you have additional drives, they are named B, C, D, and so forth.

A square block or an underline will be positioned immediately to
the right of the prompt. This is the *cursor,* a symbol that indicates
where you are on the screen or where the next character you type
will appear. On some video screens, the cursor blinks.

Typing Entries on the Keyboard

When you type characters on the keyboard, the computer usually
displays them on the video screen, although this may depend on
what the computer is doing with your entries.

The examples in this book will usually show only the characters
you are to type, and no additional characters the computer may display. For example, when it is time for you to enter a command, the
computer will display the prompt:

A>

If you enter a command such as DIR, the display might look like this:

A>DIR

However, in our examples, we will only show the characters:

DIR

that you are to type.

Whenever the computer displays the A>, you can safely enter a
command. After you type a command at the keyboard, you must
indicate to the computer that the line is complete and ready to be
processed, or *executed.* The *carriage return* key, sometimes called
simply the return key, is used for this purpose. This key may be
labeled RETURN, ENTER, or CAR RET. Sometimes the key is marked
with a bent arrow: ↵ . We will use the symbol <CR> to indicate
that you must press the return key. When you press the return key, the

computer automatically advances to the next line by sending both a carriage return and a *line feed* to your screen.

Let us gain more familiarity with the CP/M system by giving some simple commands. If the prompt is not A > but another letter, give the command:

A: <CR>

This will make drive A the current drive. Now, press only the RETURN key. The system prompt will appear again on a new line. Do this several times and notice how the computer simply repeats the prompt on the next line. We have seen that the RETURN key is used to send a command to the computer. In this instance, no actual command was given, so CP/M simply repeats the prompt. We have also seen that it is necessary to press the return key at the end of each command line. This tells the computer to execute the line. However, there is an exception.

Certain commands are given by pressing two keys—the control, or CTRL, key followed by a specific letter. These are known as control characters. In this book they are represented by the symbol ^ followed by the corresponding letter. For example, control-C will appear as ^C. Note that although video screens usually display the control symbol as ^, sometimes ↑ is used as the control symbol instead. Usually you do not need to hit the carriage return after a control character. The computer begins executing the command when the character is pressed. There is one caution: when you give the ^C command, the cursor must be at the beginning of the line. (You can move the cursor to the beginning of the line with ^X, though this will erase the line.)

We will discuss the control characters in detail later in this chapter. Now type the line:

ANYTHING <CR>

Since this is not a valid command, CP/M responds with the error message:

ANYTHING?

and then displays the system prompt again. The computer will not proceed until you enter a valid command.

If the CP/M prompt is displayed but your system fails to respond to keyboard entries, then something is wrong. You may have to press the reset button or turn off the computer and turn it back on again. Sometimes you can restart the computer by giving the ^C command.

What Not to Do When the Computer Refuses to Respond

What's Wrong?

Sometimes something unusual happens, and you are not sure what caused it. There are various things you can try.

If you press RETURN at the end of a command line and get no response from the computer, the computer may be busy doing something, such as running a program. You may have inadvertently typed the name of a program that actually exists, and CP/M has begun executing that program. Sometimes you can abort the program and return to the CP/M system by typing ^C, but not always.

If typing ^C has no effect, check to see if a disk drive light is on. This may mean that the computer is trying to read the disk in that drive. If the light is on and there is no disk in that drive, then you must start over from the beginning. If there is a disk in drive A, press the reset button to perform a cold boot. If there is no disk in drive A, shut off the computer. Then turn on the computer and go through the regular startup procedure.

CONTROL CHARACTERS

CP/M contains a set of characters, known as *control characters,* that have special meaning to the system. Two keys are required for entering each control character from the keyboard—the control key, usually marked CTRL, and a letter key.

You do not press both keys at the same time. Press the control key first and then, while holding down the control key, press the letter key (see Figure 2.1). It does not matter whether the shift lock is engaged when you enter a control character. In other words, a lowercase ^C is the same as an uppercase ^C.

The complete set of control characters includes ^A through ^Z, though not all of these characters are used by CP/M. A complete list of the CP/M control characters appears in Appendix C.

Before we discuss the uses of the control characters in CP/M, let us look briefly at the special control keys.

Special Control Keys

Some keyboards use special keys to perform the functions of frequently used control characters. The backspace is a good example. Computers usually have a key labeled BACKSPACE or marked with a left-pointing arrow. Pressing this key enters the same command as ^H, and the system responds the same way to both. Another example is the carriage return command (<CR>), which indicates to CP/M that the command line is ready to be executed. You can enter a carriage return command with ^M. However, this is unnecessary, since keyboards always have a separate return key.

Figure 2.1 – Entering Control-C(^C)

Control-C (^C)

Entering ^C produces what is called a *warm start,* or a *warm boot* (in contrast to the cold start, when you start up the system for the first time with a bootstrap load). Essentially, it interrupts whatever the computer is doing and starts the operating system over again. You will see the system prompt on the screen. The cursor must be at the beginning of the line for ^C to be interpreted as a warm start command.

The warm boot is used for two purposes. First of all, as we saw earlier, you can use it to restart the system when it is not responding to your commands. It can also be used when you change disks in a disk drive. This forces CP/M to read the directory of the new disk.

Editing a Line with the Control Characters

You may inadvertently press a wrong key or want to change something in the line you have just typed. You can use the control characters to make changes as long as you haven't pressed the carriage return yet. Figure 2.2 gives a list of the control characters used for editing. In this section, we will examine them one by one.

Type the word ANYTHING but do not press the carriage return. While holding the control key, press the H key. This is the ^H, or backspace, character. Notice that each time you give the ^H command, the cursor backs up on the video screen, erasing the previous character. You can use ^G to delete the character at the cursor position without disturbing the remainder of the line.

COMMAND	ACTION
^A	Move cursor one character left*
^B	Move cursor to beginning of line or to end of line if cursor is already at the beginning*
^E	Move cursor to next line (used for a long line)
^F	Move cursor one character right*
^G	Delete character at cursor position*
^H	Delete character to left of cursor
^I	Move cursor to next tab position
^J	Execute command (line feed)
^K	Delete from cursor to end of line*
^M	Execute command (carriage return)
^R	Redisplay line
^U	Delete all characters in line
^W	Recall previous command line*
^X	Delete all characters to left of cursor

* Indicates commands that are not available to nonbanked form of CP/M Plus

Figure 2.2 – Control Characters Used for Editing

See if you can locate a key labeled BACKSPACE or a key with a left-pointing arrow. As we saw earlier, when you press this key, it does the same thing as ^H.

You use ^H to delete a single character. Sometimes you might want to delete more than one character in a row. You can delete all the characters to the right of the cursor with ^K (for kill) and all the characters to the left of the cursor with ^X. For example, type the word ANYTHING again but do not press the carriage return. Now type ^X. That is, while holding the control key, press the X key. Notice that the cursor moves all the way back to the beginning of the line, erasing the line.

A way to erase a complete line no matter where the cursor is positioned in the line is to use ^U. Type the word ANYTHING yet another time and then press ^U. CP/M displays the number sign (#) and then moves the cursor to the beginning of the *next* line. This command tells CP/M to ignore the line, although you can still read it on the video screen.

A> ANYTHING#   (^U given)

(Ready for next command)

Typing ^W after ^U restores the canceled line, and CP/M redisplays this line as though you had just typed it. You can then edit the new command by using the other control characters, or execute the line without change simply by pressing the carriage return.

You can move the cursor back and forth through the command line without altering the existing characters. ^A moves the cursor one character to the left, and ^F moves it one character to the right. You can move the cursor directly to the beginning of the line with ^B. If the cursor is already at the beginning of the line, ^B moves it to the end of the line.

You can insert additional characters wherever the cursor is positioned simply by typing them. The remaining characters on the line are automatically shifted to the right.

You are not likely to use ^E and ^R very often. ^E moves the cursor down to the next line so you can continue typing the same command line. It is useful for a very long command line or a very narrow video screen. ^R reprints the command line on the next line.

Other Control Characters

As we will see later, you may sometimes want to stop a moving video display at a particular point. For example, you may want to stop the display before the screen has been filled or if the information is going by too quickly for you to read it. Another case concerns programs, which generally do not stop when the screen has been filled, so information is lost as it moves, or *scrolls,* off the screen.

CP/M Plus provides a means of freezing the screen at any time. Press ^S to stop the display momentarily. Then when you are ready for the listing to continue, press ^Q, and the display will resume scrolling. Frequently, you can prematurely terminate a task by pressing ^C. However, it may be necessary to freeze the screen with ^S first.

If you want your printer to produce a hard copy of what is on the video screen, you can press ^P to engage the printer and everything you type after that will be printed. We will discuss printouts further later in this chapter.

Two other control characters—the tab key, ^I, and the line feed, ^J—are not required for the operation of CP/M. However, because they are frequently used with applications programs, modern terminals often provide special keys for these characters.

Finally, ^Z marks the end of strings in certain CP/M commands. CP/M also places this character at the end of each text file. Consequently, ^Z cannot occur in a text file. (Strings and text files will be discussed in later chapters.)

Now that you are familiar with some CP/M operations, we will learn different ways to duplicate a disk by making a backup copy of the system disk.

DUPLICATING DISKS

Programs may be safely stored on disk if you are very careful in using and storing the disks. However, even when you observe all the proper precautions, it is possible to lose information stored on a magnetic disk because of events such as an unexpected power failure while the the disk is being written. Therefore, it is prudent to make backup copies of all important disks.

The System Disk

Your system disk is your most important disk, as it contains the computer's operating system. Remember that your system disk is especially designed for your particular computer, so it must not be used in a computer with different hardware. If you change any of the hardware of your system, such as the printer, the console, or the memory size, the operating system on your current system disk may not work. The steps needed to change CP/M are described in *Mastering CP/M* (SYBEX, 1983). If you do make changes in CP/M, be sure to label the different system disks so they will not get mixed up.

In the next sections we will learn two different methods for duplicating a disk. One method is longer since three separate steps are required. On the other hand, this method always works. The second method is easier and faster. However, it requires a nonstandard program that may not be available on your system.

Because your system disk is so essential, you should make a backup copy right away. You may back it up on a new disk or use an old disk by erasing any existing programs. A new disk must be properly formatted before it is used for the first time, so in the next section we will learn how to format a disk.

Formatting a Floppy Disk

Information is stored on the surface of a disk as a sequence of groups known as *blocks.* Because many different formats, or arrangements of blocks, are in use, the surface of each floppy disk must be prepared to receive information in the desired format. This preparation, known as *formatting,* must be done before a disk is used for the first time.

To begin, turn on your computer and at the A> prompt enter the keyboard command DIR and a carriage return (<CR>). The computer will list the programs stored on the system disk. Because CP/M Plus contains many programs, it is likely that all the files are not on the same system disk. When we speak of the system disk, therefore, we may actually be referring to a number of separate disks. If you don't find the program you are looking for on the first, be sure to check the others.

Now look for a program named FORMAT.COM and a program named COPY.COM. (In discussing use of these programs, we will omit the .COM because you do not type it when you enter the command.) If these names do not appear in the listing and the message:

SYSTEM FILE(S) EXIST

appears, give the command DIRSYS and look at this listing.

We have seen that, because programs depend on the CP/M system for interaction with the hardware, the same version of a program can generally be run on all CP/M computers. The formatting program is an exception. It must be specifically written for a particular computer. Do not try to format a disk on one computer with a formatting program taken from a different computer, even though both use CP/M.

Be warned that the formatting program will destroy any information previously stored on a disk. Consequently, be sure to use a new disk or one that does not contain information you want to preserve. Be careful not to accidently format your system disk. If you are in doubt, remove the system disk before you begin the actual formatting.

You can format a disk in any drive, but the usual arrangement, which we will follow, is to put your system disk in drive A and the disk to be formatted in drive B. Let us assume you have found the program called FORMAT. Give the command:

FORMAT <CR>

Sometimes FORMAT is part of COPY. If you found COPY but not FORMAT, execute COPY and select the FORMAT option.

Most computers have provisions for more than one type of format. Therefore, when the program begins executing, you may be asked whether you want double density or single density and whether the disk is double sided or single sided. Choose double density (or extended density if it is offered) and double sided. Some formatting programs require your answers to be only in uppercase letters, but most programs accept either upper or lower case. Sometimes the formatting program can operate automatically, and so there will be no questions.

At the end of the formatting, the program will ask if you want to format another disk. Take the newly formatted disk out of drive B, insert it into its envelope, and put it aside. Insert another new disk into drive B and follow the directions to format this disk also.

CP/M can record the time and date that a file was created or most recently altered. It can also record when it was last accessed or executed. This feature, called *time and date stamping,* enables you to distinguish the more recent version of two similar files. CP/M must be especially instructed to do this with the technique described in Chapter 7.

The important thing to remember is that if you want to use time and date stamping, you must specially prepare the directory before you place any files on the disk. Let us perform this step now.

Give the command:

INITDIR B: <CR>

The screen will show:

DO YOU REALLY WANT TO RE-FORMAT THE DIRECTORY: (Y/N)?

Answer Y for yes and press the return key.

The newly formatted disks can be used to create new programs or data files. However, they cannot be used in drive A since they do not contain the CP/M operating system. Let us see how to fix that.

Copying the CP/M System with COPYSYS

CP/M disks are partitioned into two regions, one containing the system tracks and the other containing the programs and data files. Part of CP/M is located on the system tracks, and part is located in a file named CPM3.SYS. Disks used in drive A should contain CP/M, but disks in other drives do not need CP/M. Of course, disks containing CP/M can be used in any drive.

We will use a program called COPYSYS.COM (COPYSYS for short) to copy both parts of the CP/M system from drive A to drive B. (Note that, in general, the terms "drive A" and "disk A" both mean "the disk in drive A.") If you are duplicating a disk that does not contain CP/M, omit this step. You still must use PIP to copy the regular files.

The copy operation is performed in two steps. The first step copies the CP/M system from drive A into memory. The second part will copy the memory version to drive B. COPYSYS must be specifically written for your computer. A version written for a different computer will not work.

With the original system disk in drive A and the newly formatted disk in drive B, give the command:

COPYSYS <CR>

As the program begins operation, it displays several lines of information on the video screen. The exact wording will be different from one computer to the next. Now you must tell the program where (from which disk) to get a copy of the system. The last line on the screen may be something like:

Source drive name (or return for default)

Enter the letter A and then press the carriage return.

Alternatively, a list of options may be presented on the screen. A cursor will be next to the default, or the line will be highlighted. If this is not your choice, move the cursor with the up or down arrows to the appropriate choice. Then press return. If your computer uses this method to execute COPYSYS, continue to follow the directions on the screen. Otherwise, continue as described below.

When the program responds with words like:

Place source on A, then type return

press the carriage return key a second time. This will direct COPYSYS to copy the CP/M system into memory from the disk in drive A. The program now displays several more lines of text. The last line is:

Destination drive name (or return to reboot)

This time type the letter B and press the carriage return. The program responds with:

Place destination disk on B, then type return

Since you have a disk in drive B, simply press the carriage return again. COPYSYS will write a copy of CP/M from memory to the system tracks of drive B.

COPYSYS then asks:

Do you wish to copy CPM3.SYS?

Type Y for yes, and COPYSYS copies this file to drive B. The cycle then repeats so you can copy the CP/M system to additional disks.

Take the new disk out of drive B and insert the first disk you formatted. Copy the system to this new disk by responding to the questions as you did before. The program will not ask about the source drive now since the information is already in memory. After the CP/M system has been copied to the second disk, the program will cycle a third time. This time respond with simply a carriage return, and the program will terminate. Control returns to CP/M.

We are now ready to copy the programs from the original system disk to the disk in drive B.

Copying the Programs and Data with PIP

Our copying procedure is nearly complete. We have formatted two new disks and copied the CP/M system tracks and the CPM3.SYS file onto them. In fact, if we needed a new empty disk for data, we would be finished. In the next step, we will copy all the programs and data files from the original disk by using a powerful program called PIP.

Be sure that the original disk is still in drive A and one of the newly formatted disks is in drive B. If your screen does not show drive A as the current drive, give the command A: <CR>. Then give the command:

PIP B: = A: *.* [V] <CR>

Be sure to insert a space after the name PIP but nowhere else. This command directs PIP to copy all the files from drive A to drive B. As each file is copied, its name is displayed on the video screen. At the end of the copying step, the CP/M prompt will appear again, and you can continue with another operation or shut off your computer. When you have finished copying disks, be sure to put each in an envelope and label it properly.

In the next section we will duplicate a disk in a different way, using a program called COPY. If you do not have such a program, skip on to the next section.

Duplicating a Disk with COPY

The programs FORMAT, COPYSYS, and PIP can be used to duplicate any disk because these are standard CP/M programs. We will now consider another method for duplicating a disk.

Duplicating disks with the program called COPY is much simpler because all three of the operations—formatting a new disk, copying the CP/M system, and copying the programs—are performed with a single command. However, COPY is not a standard CP/M program, so it may not be present on your CP/M system disk. COPY must be specifically written for your particular hardware. Do not try to use a version taken from a different computer because it will not work. If you cannot find the program COPY, skip on to the next section.

If you want to try out the COPY program, place a new unformatted disk in drive B and the system disk in drive A. (You can also use an old disk in drive B, or one of the disks formatted in the previous section.) Give the command:

    COPY <CR>

COPY will ask for the name of the source drive and the name of the destination drive. Answer with A for the source and B for the destination. Source on A and destination on B is the usual procedure, so this is usually the default option. In this case you only have to give a carriage return without specifying the drives to perform the task. With these simple commands, COPY will perform all the necessary operations to duplicate your system disk.

SOME ELEMENTARY OPERATIONS WITH PIP

PIP is a very powerful and versatile program. We already used PIP to copy all the files from one disk to another. PIP can also be used to alter a disk file, display a disk file on the console or printer, and create a disk file from the keyboard. Since Chapter 4 is devoted entirely to PIP, we will only look briefly at the more important features here.

Creating a Data File

We have previously considered disk files such as PIP and FORMAT that are provided with CP/M. However, it is also possible to create a disk file of your own. In this case the file contains ordinary text such as the letters of the alphabet. This type of disk file is known as a *text file.*

Since we are going to create a new file on drive B, be sure that there is a disk in that drive. After we have created the disk file, we will use it to demonstrate some CP/M features.

Normally, you would use PIP for copying files and use a system editor such as ED or a word processing program to create files. However, before we learn the commands necessary to use ED, we need some files to work with. We need only a very small data file, so we can create it with PIP. Keep in mind that it will not be possible to edit the file or correct errors when you are using PIP. Any characters you type, including control characters, will become part of your file, so be sure to type very carefully. On the other hand, we are not going to use the information in the file, so it doesn't matter if there are typing mistakes.

If the system does not show drive B as current, type:

    B: <CR>

Next type the command line:

    A:PIP SAMPLE.TXT = CON: <CR>

Be sure to include a space after the word PIP but nowhere else on the line.

This command directs PIP to read all characters that are typed at the console (CON:) and place them into a disk file named SAMPLE.TXT. When we used PIP earlier to duplicate disk files, the destination file name was given first, and that was followed by the source file name. A similar construction is used here, except that the source is the console keyboard rather than a disk file. Notice that there is a colon at the end of the word CON. This is a CP/M convention used to distinguish a peripheral device from a disk file. We could create a disk file with the name CON, but we would not include a colon at the end of its name.

Usually when you want to begin a new line, you type just a carriage return. CP/M then automatically adds a line feed. However, when you are entering data with PIP, you must add your own line feed after each return. The line-feed key on your terminal may be marked with a downward-pointing arrow. If you cannot find a line-feed key, use ^J, the line-feed character. In the following example, the symbol <LF> is used to remind you to enter the line feed after the carriage return.

After typing the PIP command line, enter the following two lines of text into your new file. Everything you type will be included in the new file.

> This is my new text file called SAMPLE.TXT. <CR> <LF>
> This is the second line of my new file. <CR> <LF>

Complete the operation by typing a ^Z. This command terminates PIP and returns control to CP/M. You have just created a new disk file called SAMPLE.TXT that contains the lines you typed at the keyboard.

Duplicating a Single Disk File

To be sure that you understand the operation of PIP, let us make a duplicate copy of the disk file SAMPLE.TXT. If you are not already on drive B, give the command:

> B: <CR>

Now give the command:

> A:PIP COPY.TXT = SAMPLE.TXT[V] <CR>

Be sure to insert a space after PIP but nowhere else.

This command directs PIP to make a copy of your file. The symbol V enclosed in square brackets directs PIP to verify that the new copy is correct. Always give the verification option when you are copying disk files.

DISPLAYING AND PRINTING A FILE

There are several different ways to look at a text file. Let us consider some of them.

Displaying a File on the Screen

After we created and copied a text file using PIP, we returned to the CP/M operating system. We can use the CP/M command TYPE to display the contents of the new file on the video screen.

At the system prompt enter the command:

   TYPE SAMPLE.TXT <CR>

Be sure to include a space between TYPE and SAMPLE but nowhere else.

A word of caution: you can inspect only text files, not all kinds of files, with the TYPE command. We have introduced TYPE here only as a way of seeing our new file. We will discuss this command and its limitations in detail in Chapter 3.

You can also use PIP to display a file. This method is not as convenient, but it demonstrates a general use of PIP. Give the command:

   A:PIP CON: = SAMPLE.TXT <CR>

Notice that the command is the reverse of the one we used to create the file in the first place. This command directs PIP to send the contents of the file SAMPLE.TXT to the console (CON:). Do not forget to add a colon to the end of CON, or CP/M will create a disk file named CON instead.

Now that we have seen how to display a file on the video screen, let us see how to send a file to the printer instead of the screen.

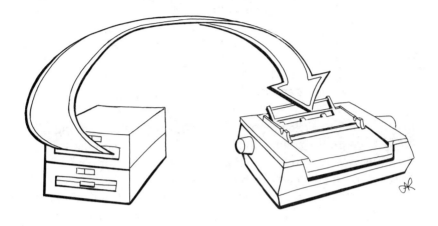

Printing a Text File

Sometimes we need to obtain a printed listing or hard-copy version of a text file. We can use PIP to send a copy to the printer. Turn on your printer and give the command:

A:PIP LST: = SAMPLE.TXT <CR>

If you make a typing error, use the control characters to correct the error.

Notice that this command is similar to the previous one except that the device name CON: (console) has been changed to LST: (list). Notice that there is a colon at the end of the name LST. This distinguishes the printer from a disk file named LST.

There is an alternative method for printing text files. It is not as sophisticated as the first method because the commands you type also appear in the printer output, but the second method is faster. Let us try it.

Be sure that the printer is turned on and give the command ^P to engage the printer. All subsequent output will appear at the printer as well as on the screen. Giving the ^P command a second time reverses the effect, disengaging the printer. In other words, ^P acts as a toggle that turns the printer alternately on and off.

Engage the printer with the ^P command. Then give the command:

TYPE SAMPLE.TXT <CR>

In this case, the TYPE command will appear at the beginning of the listing because the printer was engaged before it was typed. To prevent this, you could type ^P after typing the command line but before entering the carriage return.

After CP/M has completed printing the file, it will display the prompt B> on the video screen. This prompt will also appear in the printer output since the printer is still engaged. Give the ^P command again so that no additional characters will appear at the printer.

The TYPE command stops each time the video screen has been filled. This is convenient if you want to read the information on the screen. However, if you are using TYPE to print a long file, it would be better to print the entire file without stopping. To do this, you place what is called the NOPAGE option in brackets at the end of the TYPE command. This version of TYPE requires a program called TYPE.COM located on the system disk. Make drive A current and give the command:

TYPE B:SAMPLE.TXT [NO PAGE]

Place a space after TYPE. The spaces after TXT and NO are not required. The option can be abbreviated to [NO P if you want, omitting the right bracket.

Let us now learn about files and file names by examining the disk directory.

FILES AND FILE NAMES

A program or a collection of data can be stored on the disk as a *file*. Each file is assigned a unique *file name* that you use to refer to the file. When a file is written on disk, the CP/M operating system creates an entry in the disk *directory* to keep track of where the file is located on the disk. The directory is located on the same disk.

If you want to execute a program, you simply give CP/M the corresponding file name. CP/M will locate the program on the disk from the information contained in the disk directory. It will then copy the program into memory and execute it.

The directory of a disk is like the directory of offices in the foyer of a building, listing names and locations corresponding to the tenants of the building. If the directory is destroyed, the programs on the disk, like the offices in the building, can no longer be located.

If a program needs data to work with, you can enter the required information directly from the keyboard. Alternatively, the information may be stored in a data file on the disk, and you simply enter the name of the data file. Let us now examine the directory on disk A.

Examining the Disk Directory

In this section we will look briefly at the commands DIR and DIRSYS, which are used to examine the disk directory. Both commands are discussed in more detail in the next chapter.

The disk in drive A contains the CP/M operating system as well as programs. You can obtain a listing of the files that are present on this drive by typing the command DIR (for directory). The listing might look like this:

```
A:PIP      COM : COPY   COM : TYPE   COM : SHOW   COM
A:DUMP     COM : SID    COM : WS     COM : WSMSGS OVR
A:WSOVLY1 OVR : DEVICE  COM : SUBMIT COM : MBASIC  COM
A:SORT     BAS : SETDEF COM : DIR    COM : SET     COM
A:RMAC     COM : COPYSYS COM :
```

If you get the message:

SYSTEM FILE(S) EXIST

it means that there are additional files. You can list these files by giving the command DIRSYS after the next CP/M prompt appears.

The display in this example shows four different file names on each line. We know that these files are on the system disk in drive A because each line of the display begins with the letter A. A colon separates one file name from the next. Each file name is shown in two parts, with blank spaces separating the first part from the second part. (The output from DIR is not typical. With other CP/M programs the two parts of the name are separated by a period; for example, PIP.COM, not PIP COM.) If there are many directory entries, the display automatically stops when the screen is filled. Press the space bar to view the next screenful or give the ^C command to terminate the listing.

CP/M File Names

A CP/M file name consists of two parts—the primary name and the extension. The two parts are usually separated by a period.

The *primary name,* to the left of the period, has one to eight characters. The primary name describes the contents of the file. The *extension,* which follows the period, contains a maximum of three characters. Typically, the extension indicates the type of file, so this part of the file name is also called the *type.* For example, all files with COM as an extension are command files or programs. Files with BAS as an extension are BASIC source programs, and files with OVR and OVL as an extension are overlay files, those designed to be copied over other programs. You must not choose the extension BAK, since the system editor uses this name for backup files, or $$$, as these files are automatically erased. Text files do not have to have extensions; however, TXT is commonly used as an extension. A summary of common file-name extensions is given in Figure 2.3.

When you are naming files, be sure to make the primary name distinct from the primary names of other files. Do not simply give files the same primary names and different extensions. For example, you could name two chapters of a book CHAP1.TXT and CHAP2.TXT, but you should not name them CHAP.1 and CHAP.2. Let us see why.

When you alter a file with the system editor, the new version is automatically given the original name and the extension of the original file is changed to BAK (for backup). For example, if you edit a file named CHAP.1, the original version becomes CHAP.BAK. If you then edit CHAP.2, the original copy of this file also becomes CHAP.BAK.

Two files cannot have the same name, so the first CHAP.BAK is erased. If you name the files CHAP1.TXT and CHAP2.TXT, there will be no problem because the backup files will be named CHAP1.BAK and CHAP2.BAK.

Sometimes you must refer to a file by only its primary name and not give its extension. For example, to load the BASIC source program SORT.BAS, you only have to give the primary name SORT. As another example, all program files must have an extension of COM. However, you execute a program simply by entering the primary name. The extension must not be included.

Sometimes you must give the complete file name, including a period between the primary part and the extension. For example, if you want to display a file on the video screen with the TYPE command,

EXTENSION	TYPE OF FILE
ASM	Assembly language source file
BAK	Backup file
BAS	BASIC source program
COM	Transient program
FOR	FORTRAN source program
HEX	Hexadecimal file created by MAC
INT	Intermediate work file
LIB	Library file used by MAC and RMAC
PAS	Pascal source program
OVL	Overlay file used by other programs
OVR	Overlay file used by other programs
PLI	PL/I source program
PRN	Print file created by MAC and RMAC
REL	Relocatable file created by RMAC
SPR	System page relocatable file for CP/M
SUB	Source file used by SUBMIT
SYM	Symbol table file created by MAC and RMAC
SYS	System file used by CP/M
XRF	Cross-reference file
$$$	Temporary file

Figure 2.3 – Examples of File-Name Extensions

CP/M will not know what kind of file you have in mind. Therefore, it is necessary to give the complete name, including the extension. Similarly, you must give the complete name of a file when you want to alter it with the system editor.

Valid File-Name Characters

File names are formed from the 26 letters of the alphabet and the 10 digits. You can also use some of the special characters, such as:

+ − / % $

in any position of either the primary or the extension name. However, remember that you must not use $$$ as a file-name extension. This is a name assigned by PIP and other programs to designate intermediate results. Files with this extension are automatically erased at the conclusion of the task.

These characters:

< > . , : = ; * ? [ ] !

must not be used in a file name because they have special meaning to the CP/M system or to some of the programs, such as PIP. For example, the file name:

PROG-22.TXT

is legal, but the file name:

PROG = 22.TXT

is not because it contains the equals sign.

Ambiguous File Names

Sometimes you may need to refer to several files at once or want to locate one file in a collection of similar files. If all the files in the group have a part of their names in common, you can refer to them by a single file name known as an *ambiguous* name. As we have seen, CP/M file names contain two parts, or *fields*—the primary part and the extension. Ambiguous file names use the symbols ? or ∗ in either the primary part or the extension as a sort of "wild card." The question mark represents a single character at the given position, and the asterisk refers to all the remaining characters in the field. Let us see how ambiguous file names work.

An example of an ambiguous file name is: SORT? The computer will match this name with any file names containing SORT and one more character. For example, it will match SORT1, SORT2, and SORT3 but it will not match SORT12. It will also match SORT.

Primary names always occupy eight characters of a directory entry. If a name has fewer than eight, CP/M fills out the remaining positions with blanks. For example, the name SORT1 is five characters long, so there are three blanks at the end. The name SORT is four characters long and contains four blanks at the end. Except in the directory listing, the blanks do not appear when the name is displayed by the computer.

A blank character in a file name can match an ambiguous symbol. Therefore, the name SORT matches the ambiguous name SORT? because the fifth character of the name SORT is a blank.

When an asterisk is included in an ambiguous name, CP/M fills out the name with question marks. This is an internal change that is not shown on the screen. For example, when the ambiguous name SORT∗ is given, CP/M converts it internally to: SORT???? Therefore, the ambiguous name SORT∗ matches the file names SORT, SORT1, SORT12, SORT123, and SORT1234. The result is the same as if the name SORT???? had been given. Let us consider a few more examples.

CP/M will fill in ambiguous names in either direction. Thus, ∗.BAS is expanded internally to ????????.BAS and refers to all files with the extension BAS. The name SORT.∗ becomes SORT.??? and refers to all files with the primary name SORT no matter what the extension might be. This name also matches the file name SORT without an extension.

Notice that the asterisk only applies to one of the two fields—the primary name or the extension—but not to both. The special form ∗.∗ becomes ????????.??? and so refers to all files on the disk. There can be other characters in front of the asterisk that precedes the period but none afterward. For example, C*.BAS is correct, but *C.BAS is not. Recall that earlier we used an ambiguous file name to copy an entire disk. The command was:

   PIP B: = A: * . * [V]

The symbol *.* represented all the files on the disk. The ambiguous symbols can be used with DIR, TYPE, and PIP when you need to refer to several files.

Try using the ? and * symbol with DIR to see how ambiguous names can select groups of files. Remember the ? will match any one character for each occurrence. If drive A is not current, give the command A: <CR>. Then give the commands (all followed by <CR>):

DIR *.COM	(all COM files)
DIR S*.COM	(all COM files beginning with S)
DIR ???.COM	(COM files with three-letter primary names)
DIR S??.COM	(COM files with three-letter primary names beginning with S)
DIR WS*.*	(all WordStar files)

In the first example, the ambiguous name *.COM matches all COM files. The second example matches all COM files with S as the first character. The programs SHOW.COM, SID.COM, SUBMIT.COM, and SET.COM match this name.

The third example demonstrates use of the question mark. The ambiguous name ???.COM will match PIP.COM, SID.COM, SET.COM, and DIR.COM because each has three characters in the primary name. However, we saw that the question mark also matches a blank. Therefore, this ambiguous name will also match WS.COM because the third character is a blank. It will not match names such as SHOW.COM and SUBMIT.COM since the primary names have more than three characters.

The fourth example is like the third except that the first character must be the letter S. The files SID.COM and SET.COM match this specification. The fifth example will match all files on a WordStar disk that start with WS.

SUMMARY

In this chapter we learned about computer operating systems and became acquainted with some of the features of CP/M Plus. We have seen how CP/M responds to entries from the keyboard with particular video screen displays, and we learned to recognize and change the current, or default, disk drive. We learned the CP/M control characters and special control keys, particularly those used for editing the command line.

We formatted new disks using FORMAT and duplicated disks in several different ways, using the programs COPYSYS, PIP, and COPY.

After creating and copying a file with PIP, we learned how to display the file on both the video screen and printer. We finished the chapter by viewing the disk directory with DIR and then learning the conventions for naming files.

You may be surprised to learn that you now know enough about CP/M Plus to run most applications programs without problems. If you want to learn more about your operating system and its resources, read on. In the next chapter we will learn more about the CP/M commands and programs.

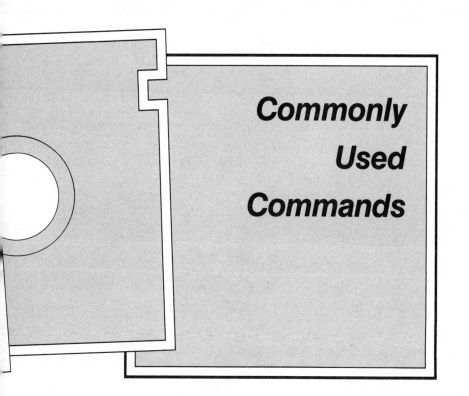

Commonly Used Commands

INTRODUCTION

In the last chapter we learned some of the basic operations of CP/M Plus. In this chapter we begin studying the system in detail. We will learn how to use the built-in commands USER, DIRSYS, RENAME, and ERASE, and the transient programs SETDEF, SHOW, SET, SUBMIT, and DEVICE. We will also learn more about the commands DIR and

TYPE, which were introduced in Chapter 2. At this point it is not necessary to memorize all of these commands. However, you should frequently review the information in Chapters 2 and 3 because it is so important. Even if you are just a casual CP/M user, you should be familiar with the following:

- The control characters ^C, ^S, ^Q, ^X, ^U, ^P, ^H
- How to duplicate complete disks
- How to copy individual files with PIP
- How to inspect the disk directory with DIR
- How to erase files with ERASE
- How to change file names with RENAME
- How to determine the remaining disk space with SHOW

The material presented in this chapter will enable you to use the most important CP/M commands. You will probably refer to this chapter frequently until you are comfortable with the system's operation and command conventions. You will then find Chapter 7, which summarizes all the CP/M Plus commands, a useful reference guide.

COMMANDS AND PARAMETERS

Before we begin a discussion of the various commands, let us consider the distinction between a command and its parameters. As we have seen, a command is an instruction that you give to CP/M in a specific form. A parameter is an item of information that qualifies the command. Usually a parameter is the name of a disk file that is going to be affected by the command.

For example, in the line:

    DIR SORT.BAS

the first word, DIR, is the command to CP/M. The second word, SORT.BAS, is the parameter, which tells CP/M to display the name SORT.BAS if the files is found in the directory. Using ambiguous characters in a parameter, such as DIR *.BAS, refers to all files with the type BAS.

Parameters may be optional or required with a particular command, depending on the situation. The discussion of each command will indicate generally when you need to add a parameter. If you omit a required prameter, CP/M will usually ask for it.

A particular kind of parameter, known as an *option,* is enclosed in square brackets. Option parameters modify the operation of a command. We previously used the V option with PIP and the NO PAGE option with TYPE. For example, the command:

    TYPE SORT.BAS[NO PAGE]

commands CP/M to display the file SORT.BAS. The output does not stop at the end of each screen or page because the NO PAGE option is included.

The file-name parameter designates the file that the command will work with. The option parameter alters the operation of the command.

File-parameters must be separated from the command itself by at least one space. Note that a space may not appear in the middle of a command or a parameter.

The beginning square bracket of the option parameter is placed immediately following the file-name parameter without an intervening space. If a file-name parameter is not given, the option parameter is placed immediately after the command, without a space. The closing square bracket is optional. Longer option parameters may be abbreviated to two or three characters.

Parameters may include letters (A–Z), digits (0–9), and other symbols. You may enter the letters as either upper case (capital) or lower case since CP/M converts all letters on the command line to upper case. The parameters given on the command line are known collectively as the *command line tail.*

Usually only one or two file-name parameters follow a CP/M command. However, there is no limit to the number of file-name and option parameters that might be given to a CP/M command. If a line becomes too long for the video screen, type a ^E to start a new line. This moves the cursor to the beginning of the next line but does not otherwise affect the command line.

BUILT-IN COMMANDS AND TRANSIENT PROGRAMS

When CP/M displays the system prompt, you can respond with one of two types of command. One type is built into the CP/M system. We will refer to this as a *built-in command*. The other type, which we will call a *transient command* or program, is stored on disk.

The built-in commands are always present in memory during command input. Since they do not have to be copied from disk, they can be executed rapidly. Because the memory space alloted to the built-in commands is limited, there are only six such commands.

Additional operations are provided by programs that are stored on disk as command, or COM, files. You execute such a program by giving the primary name on the command line without the COM extension. In response CP/M copies the program from disk into memory and then runs the memory version. Since the memory copy is only temporary, such a program is sometimes called a transient program or transient command. The region of memory where these programs are executed is called the *transient program area* (TPA). This is the largest portion of memory.

Transient programs can be copied from one disk to another, and they can be renamed or erased. Unlike a built-in program, which is always ready to run, a transient program cannot be run until it is located on a disk.

With earlier versions of CP/M there was a clear-cut distinction between the built-in commands and the transient programs. However, with CP/M Plus that distinction has become blurred. Four of the built-in commands have transient extensions that are COM files.

CP/M automatically executes a transient extension if it needs the additional features the extension provides. Therefore, these four commands sometimes behave like built-in commands and at other times like transients.

The six built-in commands are listed below. They do not have to be spelled out in full; you can shorten them to the abbreviations listed.

COMMAND	ABBREVIATED NAME	FUNCTION
DIR	DIR	Display the disk directory
DIRSYS	DIRS	Display the directory of system files

ERASE	ERA	Erase a disk file
RENAME	REN	Rename a disk file
TYPE	TYP	Display a text file on the console
USER	USE	Change the user area

Two of these commands—DIRSYS and USER—are wholly built-in; they do not have transient counterparts. The other four commands exist as both built-in commands and transient programs. If you look at a directory listing of your system disk, the programs named DIR.COM, ERASE.COM, RENAME.COM, and TYPE.COM represent the transient versions of these commands. Because they are wholly built-in, DIRSYS and USER do not appear in the directory listing.

There is an additional built-in command that changes the default drive. If the current drive is A and you enter the command B:, CP/M will change the default drive to B.

You can add the drive name to the file name of a transient program to indicate which disk the program is located on. For example, A:PIP tells CP/M to look for PIP on disk A. The drive name is not properly a part of the file name since it is not encoded into the directory listing. By contrast, you must not add a drive name to a DIRSYS and USER command because these built-in commands are not executed from a disk file. For example, the command A:USER is improper.

If RENAME, ERASE, or TYPE are given without a file-name parameter, or if DIR, ERASE, or TYPE are given with an option parameter, the corresponding transient extension is needed. Then the transient version must be located on the current drive or the drive name must be included in the command. For example, if B is the current drive and the transient extension TYPE.COM is located on drive A, the command:

    A:TYPE SORT.BAS[NO PAGE]

is proper. Alternatively, make drive A current and give the command:

    TYPE B:SORT.BAS[NO PAGE]

As shown in the previous example, a drive name can appear in one of the parameters to a built-in command.

Now let us look at each of the six built-in commands in detail. We begin with TYPE.

TYPE

Viewing the Contents of a Text File   We have seen that the TYPE command provides an easy method for examining a text file on the video screen. To understand more about TYPE, let us look briefly at the difference between text and binary files.

Information is stored in memory or on disk as a sequence of digits. The computer also communicates with the console and the printer in digital form. However, there are several very different coding schemes used to represent digital information. Two of the most common are known as *ASCII* and *binary.* Though both of these schemes are used for information stored in memory and on disk, the console and printer are designed only for the ASCII representation.

Text files are written in ASCII, and so they can be viewed on the console or printer with the TYPE command. However, binary files, such as those with the file extension COM or REL, must first be translated to ASCII. Consequently, you cannot use the TYPE command to view these files. We will look further at the difference between text and binary files in Chapter 4.

The format for the TYPE command is:

TYPE d:name.extension

where the letter d stands for the drive name. You may omit the drive name if the file is on the default drive. If you omit the parameter with this command, CP/M will ask for it. If the file name contains the ? or * ambiguous characters, CP/M will display all the corresponding files.

Normally, CP/M will stop the display when the screen has filled. At this time, you can display the next screenful by pressing the space bar. You can obtain a continuous listing of a file by including the option NO PAGE in square brackets. For example, the command:

TYPE SORT.BAS[NO PAGE]

will display the entire file SORT.BAS without stopping when the screen is full. You can momentarily stop the display with ^S and resume it with ^Q. This method is useful for quickly surveying a file.

If you want a printed listing of a file, turn on the printer and press ^P before completing the TYPE command. Be sure to include the NO PAGE option so the printout will not stop at each page. The file will be displayed on both the video screen and the printer.

Displaying a single, unambiguous file requires only the built-in version of TYPE. However, if the ambiguous ? and * symbols are included, if the file-name parameter is omitted, or if an option parameter is given, the transient version of TYPE is required. Then TYPE.COM must be on the current disk or you must include the drive name by entering, for example, A:TYPE.

USER

Changing the User Area   Each CP/M disk can be partitioned into 16 regions, or areas, which are numbered from 0 to 15. Each area can be assigned to a different user or to a different subject. For example, you can keep formatting programs in one user area, BASIC programs in a second area, office memos in a third area, and so forth. This is a useful technique if you are working with a hard disk because it contains so much space. However, the space on a floppy disk is limited. Therefore, it is not practical to partition a floppy disk into more than a few regions, although unused space is not actually assigned to any user area.

Whenever you create a disk file, the corresponding directory entry is automatically coded with the current user number. The files in one user area are not normally accessible to those working in other user areas. (We will learn how to copy files from one user area to another in Chapter 4.)

Each time you start up CP/M, the system automatically selects user area 0. You can readily change to a different user area by giving the command USER and a parameter corresponding to the new user area. Let us see how this works. Give the command:

    USER 5 <CR>

to change to user area 5. Be sure to include a space between the command and its parameter. When the user number is not 0, CP/M displays the user number in the prompt. For example, the prompt 5A> indicates that user 5 and drive A are active. A single command can change both the user area and the default drive. For example, the command USER 3B: makes user 3 and drive B active. Try this command now (don't forget the colon).

The built-in commands are available to all user areas. However, each user normally has access to only those disk files in the current user area. Give the command:

    DIR <CR>

The response will be NO FILE because there will not be any files in user area 3. Now give the command:

    USER 0 <CR>

to return to your original user area 0. Give the DIR command to see what files you now have available.

Programs needed in several user areas can be made accessible to all users if they are designated as system files in user area 0. The SET program discussed later in this chapter is used for that purpose.

Certain programs, such as as FORMAT and COPY, can destroy useful information if they are used incorrectly. If these programs are stored in a separate user area, there is less likelihood that they will be executed accidentally.

DIR

Listing the Directory   The DIR command was introduced in Chapter 2, where we used it to determine the names of files stored on drive A. Now let us study the command in more detail. The DIR command has both a built-in and a transient version. DIR can display a list of all files, a list of selected files, or a single file on any disk.

The command DIR given without a parameter displays all the files of the current user on the current disk. Sometimes the directory contains so many names that the video screen is completely filled. When this happens, CP/M automatically stops the display. You can continue the listing by pressing the space bar, or you can terminate the listing by pressing ^C.

There are two ways to list the directory of a drive that is not current. One method is to give the drive name as a parameter to the DIR command. For example, to display the names of all files located on drive B when drive A is current, give the command:

    DIR B: <CR>

Be sure to include the colon after the letter B and leave a space after DIR but nowhere else. If you omit the colon, CP/M will look for a disk file named B.

An alternative method of viewing the B directory is first to make drive B current and then to give the DIR command without a parameter. The commands are:

    B: <CR>
    DIR <CR>

The first method is quicker, and you remain in drive A at the end of the step. The second method requires an extra command, and you remain on drive B when the DIR command has finished.

You can obtain a permanent listing of the directory by turning on the printer and typing ^P before completing the DIR command. When the listing has finished, press ^P a second time to disengage the printer.

Now let us see how to add parameters to the DIR command. We have already learned how to use file-name parameters. Let us look at a few more examples.

Adding File-Name Parameters to DIR   We have been using DIR without a file-name parameter to show all files in the listing. It is possible to limit the display to one class of files or to a single file by including a file name parameter. For example, the command:

    DIR *.COM

will display the names of all files on the current disk that have the type COM. We can use the double asterisk with DIR to display all files.

However, as we have seen, this parameter is unnecessary since it has the same result as no parameter at all.

To search for a specific file on drive B, give the file name as a parameter. For example, the command:

DIR B:SPECIFIC.BAS

will display the file name SPECIFIC.BAS if it exists on drive B. If the file does not exist, CP/M will give an error message.

A transient extension to DIR called DIR.COM can perform many additional tasks, such as placing the file names in alphabetical order and indicating the size of each file. This program must be located on the current disk or on a disk in the file-search path so that CP/M can find it. (Setting up a file-search path is discussed later in this chapter.) CP/M executes the transient version of DIR whenever options are included with the command. If CP/M cannot find DIR.COM, it will give the error message:

DIR COM REQUIRED

Remember, DIR.COM is a separate program on one of the disks. If it is located on drive A but drive B is current, you can give the command:

A:DIR[options]

It is possible to include several file names as parameters to DIR. Use a space to separate each file name from the next. Then you must specifically reference the transient version by including the drive name before DIR or adding an option such as [FULL] or [DIR]. For example:

A:DIR *.COM *.SUB

Using Options with DIR   Eighteen different options can be given to DIR. (See chapter 7 for a complete list.) However, only one or two of them are usually needed at any time. Furthermore, some of these options are mutually exclusive. The options to DIR are enclosed in a single pair of square brackets. If more than one option is given, spaces or commas are used as separators. You can abbreviate an option to the first two letters if the spelling is unique. Be careful not to confuse the DIR options with the regular file-name parameters. Let us see what the difference is.

An option to DIR is a parameter. However, it is distinguished from the file-name parameter by being enclosed in square brackets. For example, the command:

DIR SIZE

refers to the particular disk file named SIZE. However, the command:

DIR[SIZE]

creates a listing of all file names with the corresponding file sizes.

You can give both a file-name parameter and an option parameter in the same command. Either parameter can be given first. For example, the two commands:

DIR[SIZE]*.COM

and

DIR *.COM[SI

are functionally the same. They both list all COM files with their corresponding sizes in kilobytes. Notice that the second example uses the abbreviated form and that the closing square bracket is omitted. You can omit the closing bracket of an option if it will be the last item on the line.

When you give any option to the DIR command, a summary at the end of the listing shows the number of files and the total number of bytes used by the files. In addition, the files are presented in alphabetical order across each line. This can be useful when you are looking for a particular file name in a long list. However, there is a disadvantage to this feature. The ordering of the files is performed by a separate sorting routine. When there are many files in the listing, it takes CP/M a noticeable amount of time to perform the sorting.

If you are interested in determining the actual order of the file names in the directory, you may want to omit the ordering. In this case, you would use the NOSORT option. For example, the command:

DIR[SIZE,NOSORT]

lists all files in the order they occur in the disk directory and also gives the size of each file. In addition, a summary is given at the end of the listing.

Another useful option is EXCLUDE. This option displays all directory entries that do *not* match the given file-name parameter. For example, the command:

DIR *.BAK [EXCLUDE]

will list all files except those with the extension BAK.

We saw that DIR will display files on the default drive if no drive parameter is given. To determine the files on a particular drive, you can give the disk drive as a file-name parameter. There is yet another possibility. You can use the DRIVE option to determine the files on a selected drive, several selected drives, or all drives. This option takes three forms:

[DRIVE = B]
[DRIVE = (B,C,D)]
[DRIVE = ALL]

For example, to locate the disk file SAMPLE.TXT when you are not sure what drive it is on, give the command:

DIR SAMPLE.TXT [DRIVE = ALL] <CR>

Earlier we saw that a disk can be divided into several different user areas. A user in one area does not normally have access to programs belonging to other user areas. Consequently, the DIR listing shows only those programs associated with the current user number. However, it is possible to look at the directory of other user areas by including the USER option in the DIR command. There are three slightly different forms for this option. They are:

[USER = 3]
[USER = (2,3,4)]
[USER = ALL]

The first form shows the directory for user 3 even if the current user number is not 3. The second form displays the directory for users 2, 3, and 4, and the third form gives the directory for all users on the disk.

It is important to remember that the USER option to DIR is different from the USER command, which we discussed earlier in this chapter.

Before we consider the next DIR option, let us take a moment to learn about file attributes.

File Attributes We have seen that the entry recorded in the directory for each disk file contains the file name, the user number, and the file size. The directory also includes other information, known as the *file attributes*. A disk file can be marked as read only or read/write, and it can be designated as a system file or a directory file. These file attributes are initially set to read/write and directory status, but they can be changed at any time with the SET command. We will discuss SET later in this chapter.

Important files should be protected from accidental deletion by marking them as read only. However, if you want to be able to change a file with the system editor, ED, the file must be set to read/write status.

For large-capacity disks it is convenient to designate frequently used files as system files. They can be executed simply by typing the primary name in the usual way, but they do not show in the DIR listing. Another advantage is that system files located in user area 0 are accessible to all user areas. Thus, it is not necessary to have additional copies of such programs in each user area.

System files do not appear in the listing when the DIR command is given without options, but they can be displayed with the DIR option or with the DIRSYS command, which is discussed later.

Determining File Attributes with DIR There are several options to the DIR command that you can use to determine file attributes.

The option FULL will display the attributes for one file or a group of files. The listing shows all files that match the file-name parameter. For example, the command:

DIR *.COM [FULL]

lists all COM files in alphabetical order and displays the file attributes. Each line of the listing includes a file name and the appropriate symbols DIR or SYS and RW or RO. The symbols are defined as follows:

SYMBOL	MEANING
SYS	System file
DIR	Directory file
RO	Read-only file
RW	Read/write file

Note that two mutually exclusive pairs are shown. That is, a file will have either the system or the directory attribute but not both. Also, a file can be either read/write or read only but not both.

Another way to determine the attributes is to use the options DIR or SYS and RW or RO in place of the FULL option. This method shows only those files that satisfy the options. For example, the command:

    DIR *.COM [SYS RO]

displays only those system files that are marked as read-only.

We have discussed only some of the DIR options in this chapter. A complete list of the options is included with the DIR command in Chapter 7. Use the DIR command often to check which files are present on the disk. You should also check the directory after you create or erase a file to be sure that CP/M did what you wanted.

Let us now see how to display the directory of system files with a built-in command.

DIRSYS

Listing the Directory of System Files   We have just learned that system files do not appear in a DIR listing unless you use the SYS or FULL option. However, DIR gives the message:

    SYSTEM FILE(S) EXIST

when appropriate to indicate the presence of system files. When this message appears, you can use the DIRSYS command to get a listing of the system files. You may include file-name parameters (but not option parameters) with the DIRSYS command just as for the DIR command. For example, the command:

    DIRSYS *.OVR

will list all system files that have the OVR extension.

RENAME

Renaming Files   We reference files stored on disk by using their file names. Therefore, it is important to choose file names carefully. For example, it is logical to use the name FORTRAN for the FORTRAN program and the name COPY for the copy program. However, frequently file names are not very descriptive. For example, Microsoft FORTRAN is known as F80 and the CP/M copy program is called PIP. In such cases we can change the name of a file for our own use with the CP/M built-in command RENAME. This command does not alter the file in any way; it only changes the name that is listed in the disk directory.
   The format is:

    RENAME NEW = OLD

where OLD is the original file name and NEW is the new name. Notice that two file-name parameters are given. The new name comes first and the original name second, with an equals sign between the two. Be sure to include a space after RENAME. You can also put spaces on either side of the equals sign, but this is optional. You may omit the parameters, and CP/M will ask for them. RENAME.COM is required in this case.
   If the file is on the current disk, you can omit the drive name from both parameters. Otherwise, you must give the drive name with either file name or with both names. If two drive names are given,

they must agree. The following three forms are valid for renaming a disk file on drive B:

```
RENAME B:FILE.BAK = FILE.TXT
RENAME FILE.BAK = B:FILE.TXT
RENAME B:FILE.BAK = B:FILE.TXT
```

Alternatively, you can change the default drive to the one containing the file and then give the RENAME command without including a drive name.

If CP/M cannot find the original file name (the second parameter), it displays the error message NO FILE. Two different files on the same disk cannot both have the same name. Therefore, if you try to rename a file to an existing name, CP/M will ask if you want to delete the original. Let us see how you can do this.

Suppose that there are two files, named SAMPLE.TXT and SAMPLE.BAK. You want to copy a new version of SAMPLE.TXT from another disk. But first you want to delete the file SAMPLE.BAK and rename the original file SAMPLE.TXT as SAMPLE.BAK. One way to do this is to erase SAMPLE.BAK and then rename SAMPLE.TXT as SAMPLE.BAK. However, it is not necessary to erase the backup file as a separate step. CP/M will do that for you during the renaming step. Simply give the command:

```
RENAME SAMPLE.BAK = SAMPLE.TXT <CR>
```

CP/M will ask for verification that you want to delete the existing file. After the command is executed, you can use PIP to copy the file from another disk.

The transient extension RENAME.COM is required when you omit the parameters or when you use the ambiguous symbols ? and * to rename a group of files. These symbols must be used with care. They must appear in identical places in both file names. For example, all text files can be renamed to backup files with the command:

```
RENAME *.BAK = *.TXT
```

However, the command:

```
RENAME *.BAK = SORT.TXT
```

is incorrect because the ambiguous symbol does not appear in both names.

ERASE

Deleting Files Since the storage space on a disk is limited, all of it may eventually be occupied by files. Therefore, it is sometimes necessary to delete files you no longer need. The built-in command ERASE deletes a single disk file or a group of files. The format is:

    ERASE d:name

where d is an optional drive name. If the file name is omitted, CP/M will ask for it. In this case the transient version ERASE.COM is needed.

The ambiguous characters ? and * may be used (carefully) in the file name. For example, the command:

    ERASE PROG.TXT

will erase the single file PROG.TXT on the current drive. The command:

    ERASE PROG.*

will erase all files that have the primary name PROG—for example, PROG.TXT, PROG.BAK, and PROG.BK2. If you want to erase all files on a disk, give the double asterisk (*.*) as a parameter. Be sure to include a space after the command ERASE. The transient version, ERASE.COM, is required when an ambiguous character is used.

Be careful when you use the ERASE command because an accidental error can cause serious problems. For example, you can delete all backup files with the command:

    ERASE *.BAK

If you inadvertently type *.BAS instead, it will delete all BASIC files rather than all backup files.

If CP/M cannot find a file to match the parameter of ERASE, it displays the error message NO FILE.

Whenever ambiguous symbols are included in the file name, there is a potential for disaster, since several files can be erased at one time. Therefore, CP/M requests verification by repeating the command. For example, if you give the command:

ERASE *.BAS

CP/M responds:

ERASE *.BAS (Y/N)?

You must answer with a Y if you want CP/M to continue with the command. Otherwise, CP/M terminates the operation without further action.

Though CP/M asks for verification when ambiguous parameters are included in the file name, it asks only once even when there are several files to be deleted. You can add an extra margin of safety by including the option parameter CONFIRM (which can be abbreviated to C). Then CP/M will request permission to erase each individual file name. The transient version, ERASE.COM, is required. For example, the command:

ERASE *.BAK [CONFIRM]

will erase all backup files but ask specifically about each one in turn.

You can protect disk files from accidental erasure by setting the RO attribute, which is discussed later in this chapter in the section on SET. If you attempt to erase a protected file with the ERASE command, CP/M will refuse to perform the operation and will display an error message. If you want to erase a file that is already set to RO, you will first have to change it to RW with the SET command.

Now that we have learned to use the built-in commands, let us go on to the important transient programs SETDEF, SHOW, SET, SUBMIT, and DEVICE.

FIVE IMPORTANT TRANSIENT PROGRAMS

In this section, we will look at five of the most important transient programs. Though all the transient programs always have the COM file-name extension, we execute these programs by typing only the primary part of the name. The COM extension is never given in the command. For example, earlier we executed PIP.COM by typing simply the primary name PIP.

It is easy to confuse the built-in programs with the transients since both are executed similarly. You must always be aware of the difference. Remember that CP/M has only six built-in programs; all other programs are transient. You can execute a built-in program from any disk and any user area. However, if you want to execute a transient program that is not located on the current disk, you must include the drive name with the file name. If CP/M cannot find a requested transient program, CP/M repeats the name and adds a question mark.

There are two way of helping CP/M find transient programs. Earlier in this chapter we saw that transient programs can be declared as system files and stored in user area 0. These programs will then be available to all user areas on the same disk. The second method uses the command SETDEF.

SETDEF

Establishing a Search Path   It is usually convenient to keep all transient programs on a single disk—say, drive A—but make another disk—say, B—the current drive. Then it is necessary to add a drive name to each transient command. For example, if drive B is current and you want to create a file on this drive with WordStar, a transient program located on drive A, the command is:

    A:WS REPORT.TXT

Notice that you must specify the drive in the transient command since B is the current drive.

However, CP/M Plus provides a mechanism for more easily locating transient programs. The program SETDEF establishes a search path so that CP/M will automatically look for a transient program on another drive or on a sequence of drives without having to be told.

Each time you turn on your computer, you will want to execute SETDEF with a drive parameter. For example, the command:

    SETDEF A:

directs CP/M to look on drive A for any transient program unless you have specified a drive. Of course, drive A must be current when this command is given because SETDEF.COM is on drive A. Additional drives can also be specified in this command. With SETDEF, the asterisk is used to indicate the current drive. For example, the command:

    SETDEF A:, *

directs CP/M to look first on drive A and if the transient program cannot be found, to look on the current drive.

SETDEF can perform several other operations in addition to establishing a search path. These are summarized in Chapter 7.

SHOW

The transient program SHOW can reveal many different aspects of disks. We will consider only three features in this chapter—finding the remaining disk space, determining the active user numbers, and determining the remaining directory space. Before we describe the SHOW program, let us consider how information is stored on a disk.

CP/M Records and Blocks   CP/M stores information on disk in 128-byte units called *records*. Each record has a unique track and sector number. However, the disk directory references a larger unit known as a *block* or *group,* each assigned a unique block number.

The block is the smallest amount of disk space a file can occupy. Small disks use a block size of 1,028 bytes, or 1K bytes for short. Each 1K-byte block can hold a maximum of eight records, each containing 128 bytes. There may be fewer. For example, a very small file might require only one sector, or 128 bytes. CP/M would allocate a 1K block for this file nevertheless.

Larger disks use larger block sizes that contain 2K, 4K, 8K, or 16K bytes. Of course, larger blocks can contain more records. On the other hand, if the block size is 16K bytes, then even the smallest file takes up 16K bytes.

Now let us see how to obtain more information about disk files using the program SHOW.

Determining the Remaining Disk Space   We have seen that the DIR command can produce a listing of the disk directory. Furthermore, when the options FULL or SIZE are included in the command, the size of each file, the total space occupied by the file, and the number of records are shown. However, DIR does not give the remaining disk space. It is important to have this information. As you create more and more programs on a disk, all of the available space will be used up. You must be careful not to continue working on a disk when there is no more room. Otherwise, you can lose the program you are working on. You can use the program SHOW to determine the remaining disk space.

To use SHOW, we must first understand the principle of resetting disks. Each time a disk is first accessed, CP/M reads the disk directory and makes a copy in memory. On subsequent accesses to this disk,

CP/M assumes that the disk has not been changed and therefore does not read the disk directory again. Typing ^C resets the disks so that the directory will be read at the next access. You can observe this action by going to each disk in turn. For example, go to drive A, give the ^C command, then go to drive B. This drive will start up as CP/M reads the directory. Go back to drive A and then return to drive B. The drive will not start up this time. We say that the ^C command *resets* or *logs out* the disks. A drive is *logged in* when CP/M reads the directory. Now let us see how to use SHOW.

First, you must find which disk SHOW is located on. Because SHOW is a system file, it should be located on the system disk in drive A. Make sure A is the current drive and then give the ^C command to reset the disks. Drive A may turn on as CP/M reads the disk directory. Give the command:

SHOW <CR>

If SHOW is located on this disk, CP/M will copy it into memory and execute it. If CP/M cannot find the program named SHOW.COM, it responds with the error message SHOW? This message means that SHOW is not on the current disk or that you misspelled the name. Be sure that your system disk containing SHOW.COM is located in drive A, that you are on drive A, and that you have typed the name SHOW correctly.

When SHOW is executed without a parameter, it reports the remaining free space for the currently logged-in drives. Since only drive A is currently logged in, the response will be something like:

A: RW, SPACE: 144K

The letter A at the beginning of the line means that the information refers to drive A. The RW symbol means that the disk currently has a read/write status; that is, it is possible to both read from and write onto the disk. SPACE: 144K indicates that 144 kilobytes of space remain on the disk (actually 144 times 1,024 bytes).

After SHOW has reported the condition of drive A, go to drive B by typing:

B: <CR>

Drive B should start up as CP/M reads the directory of this disk. Give the SHOW command again. If you have not established a search path with SETDEF, you must include the drive name A at the beginning of the file name, since SHOW is on drive A but drive B is now the default drive. In other words, the command would be:

    A: SHOW

In response to the command, SHOW will include information about disks A and B since both drives are logged in. For example, SHOW might display the following:

    A: RW, SPACE: 144K
    B: RW, SPACE: 166K

If you have more than two drives, go to each in turn and execute SHOW. You will see that the response always includes all the currently logged-in disks.

Return to drive A and give the SHOW command. This time, all the logged-on drives are reported. Type ^C to reset the disks and give the SHOW command again. This time, SHOW reports on only drive A since all of the other disks have been logged out.

Now let us look at a second feature of SHOW.

Locating the Active User Areas   We have seen that the current user does not normally have access to files in other user areas. Therefore, although the DIR command can display the names of disk files located in the current user area, it does not show what files are present in other user areas of the disk unless the USERS option is given.

Suppose that you want to run a program located on a particular disk, but you do not know what user area it is located in. If you use SHOW with the option USERS, it can identify the current user number and also list active user numbers on the disk. The option can be abbreviated to the letter U. In addition, SHOW indicates how many files belong to each user. As usual, the option is enclosed in square brackets. For example, the command:

    SHOW B: [USERS]

might produce the listing:

```
Active User : 0
Active Files: 0 1 2
B: # of files: 24 3 1
B: Number of free directory entries: 36
B: Number of time/date directory entries: 16
```

to indicate that the current user is 0, who has 24 files on drive B. User 1 has 3 files, and user 2 has 1 file. The fourth line of the display indicates that there are 36 remaining spaces in the directory for additional entries. We will look at directory space in the next section. The last line will appear only if time and date tagging have been activated (see the SET command in Chapter 7).

Two other options with SHOW are DRIVE and LABEL. DRIVE produces a listing of the disk characteristics, including total capacity, directory space, and block size. The LABEL option is used to display the unique name that can be assigned to each disk. An error message is given if no name has been assigned.

Determining the Remaining Directory Space The space available on each disk is limited in two ways. One limit is the total storage space that can be used by programs. We just learned that the program SHOW can be used to determine the remaining disk space. A second limitation is set by the directory size. A maximum number of directory entries are allowed for each different disk. This number varies from one type of disk to another. However, the maximum number is always a power of two, such as 32, 64, or 128.

When a program is written to a disk, for example by copying with PIP, the directory entry records the name, user number, and location. Large programs may require additional directory entries called *extents* to keep track of all the parts.

Directory space is limited. When all the directory entries have been used, there is no room to record additional names. Some programs, such as PIP, stop operations and display an error message when there is no directory space, whereas others may ignore this aspect and give unpredictable results.

When you are working on a disk, you should frequently use SHOW to determine that you are not running out of space. There are several ways to determine the remaining directory space. The next to last line in the previous SHOW listing illustrates one way. This line gives the number of remaining entries. You may have noticed a second method.

When you enter the DIR command with option parameters, a summary is given at the end of the listing. This includes the number of bytes, records, and blocks and the number of files shown in the listing. In addition, two numbers separated by a slash give the number of used directory entries and the number of available entries. To recall this method, make drive A current and enter the command:

   DIR[SIZE]

SET

SET is a transient program that can perform several different tasks. The most important use is changing the file attributes read only or read/write and system or directory. You can also set an entire disk to read only or read/write status. In addition, you can assign a symbolic name and password to each disk and individual passwords to each file in order to reduce the possibility of unauthorized use.

Changing the File Attributes   Earlier in this chapter we learned how to determine the file attributes read only or read/write and directory or system using the DIR command with options. Now let us see how to change these attributes with the SET command.

The command line tail used to change the attributes is the same as that used with DIR to determine the attributes. For example, the command:

   DIR *.COM[SYS,RO]

displays a listing of all COM files that are marked as both system files and as read-only files. The command:

   SET *.COM[SYS,RO]

will designate all COM files as system files and as read-only files. As with DIR, the four options are SYS, DIR, RO, and RW. Notice that only two of the four attributes can be set at a time since RO and RW are mutually exclusive, as are SYS and DIR.

Designating a Disk as Read Only We have seen that setting the RO attribute will protect individual files or groups of files from accidental erasure. A special indicator, or *flag,* is set in the directory when a file is designated RO. Sometimes it may be more convenient to set an entire disk to read-only status. You do this by omitting the file name from the command and giving just the drive name. For example, the command:

SET B:[RO]

indicates that all the files on drive B are write protected. Note that this is a temporary designation; no change is made to the directory. The disk is automatically reset to read/write status at the next warm start. Let us see how this works.

Set drive B to read-only status with the above command. Then execute SHOW. You will see that drive A has read/write status, but drive B is read only. Give the ^C command to reset the disks and then execute SHOW with the B: parameter. The results now show drive B to be read/write again. In other words, ^C has returned drive B to read/write status.

Assigning a Disk Label Because floppy disks can be removed from the drives, it is easy to get them mixed up. One way to avoid this potential problem is to assign a name or label to each. Suppose, for example, there are five staff members in an office and each has a separate disk for correspondence. It would be logical to assign the name of each member to the corresponding disk. You can do this with SET.

Disk labels follow the same rules as file names. Letters of the alphabet and the ten digits can be used. The primary name can contain up to eight characters. The optional extension can have as many as three characters. For example, the command:

SET B:[NAME = JONES]

uses the NAME option to assign the label JONES to the disk in drive B. Of course, if D is the default drive, the drive letter may be omitted from the command.

The assigned label does not appear in the DIR listing even when the FULL option is given. However, the label can be displayed with the LABEL option of SHOW. (LABEL can be abbreviated to simply L.) For example:

SHOW B:[LABEL]

displays the label assigned to the disk in drive B.

In the next sections we consider password protection of files. If you do not need to prevent others from accessing your files, you can skip this discussion.

Assigning a Disk Password   The possibility of unauthorized access to a disk file can be reduced by assigning a password to each file. But first it is necessary to assign a password to the entire disk. Let us see how to do this. (Again, remember that you can omit the drive letter if B is the default drive.)

The command:

SET B:[PASSWORD = ORION]

assigns the password ORION to the disk in drive B. If a symbolic label has not been previously assigned, CP/M will automatically choose the unimaginative name LABEL.

If you attempt to change the disk label or disk password after a password has been assigned, CP/M will ask for the password. You must give the correct password at this point, or CP/M will not make the change. Note that when you enter the password in response to this question, the password does not appear on the screen.

It is very important to realize that if you forget the password, there is *no way* to retrieve it from the system. Be sure to keep a separate record of any passwords you assign so you don't risk losing access to your files.

Password protection is removed with the command:

SET B:[PASSWORD =]

That is, the password option is given without a value.

After assigning a password to the disk, it is necessary to activate file protection before assigning passwords to individual files. The command:

    SET B:[PROTECT = ON]

activates this feature. The value OFF instead of ON deactivates this feature. Again, CP/M asks you to supply the password in order to execute the command.

Assigning File Passwords After a disk has been assigned a password and the protection option has been turned on, it is possible to protect individual files on the disk. The command is similar to the one for disk protection. For example, the command:

    SET SORT.BAS[PASSWORD = SORT]

assigns the password SORT to the file SORT.BAS.

Setting the Mode of Protection Four different modes of password protection can be selected with the PROTECT option. For example:

    SET SORT.BAS[PROTECT = READ]
    SET SORT.BAS[PROTECT = WRITE]
    SET SORT.BAS[PROTECT = DELETE]
    SET SORT.BAS[PROTECT = NONE]

sets the type of protection for SORT.BAS. When you choose READ, the default option, the password is required to read the file (with TYPE), alter the file (with ED), copy the file (with PIP), or rename the file (with RENAME). When you rename a file with a password, the password remains with the file. This is not true when you copy a file with PIP.

If you select the WRITE option, the password is not needed to display or copy the file, but it is needed to alter or rename it. The DELETE option requires a password only for deletion of the file. The NONE option removes password protection.

If a password is needed, CP/M may automatically ask for it. If CP/M doesn't request the password, enter it immediately after the file name, with a semicolon separating the two. For example, if the password for SORT.BAS is PASS, you can examine the file SORT.BAS with the command:

    TYPE SORT.BAS;PASS

SUBMIT

Executing Commands from a Disk File   Up to now we have given all our commands to CP/M by entering the information from the console keyboard. This is a convenient technique for entering one command at a time. However, sometimes it is necessary to give a sequence of commands or to repeat a command several times. In such cases, you can write the commands into a disk file and then direct CP/M to execute the commands directly from this file instead of from the keyboard. The result is the same as if the commands were entered from the keyboard.

In this section we will learn how to use the transient program SUB-MIT to execute a sequence of commands that are stored in a disk file. This technique is called *batch processing.*

To process batch commands with SUBMIT, you write the commands into a disk file that has the file extension SUB. One precaution—the disk must not be full because SUBMIT uses working space on the disk during the batch processing.

Let us investigate the operation of SUBMIT with a simple example. We will begin by using the PIP program to create a short file, which we will call TEST.SUB. (If you know how to use the system editor, ED, which we will discuss in Chapter 5, you can use it instead of PIP to create the file.) Be sure to type your information very carefully as you cannot correct mistakes with PIP.

If you are not already in drive A, go there and give the command:

    PIP TEST.SUB = CON: <CR>

then type the three lines:

    DIR <CR><LF>
    DIR B: <CR><LF>
    DIR[FULL] <CR><LF>

Recall that the symbol <LF> means you must press the line-feed or down-arrow key after the carriage return.

Next, type a ^Z to terminate PIP and return to CP/M. Inspect the new file with the command:

TYPE TEST.SUB <CR>

If you find an error, you can correct it with ED or re-create the file with PIP. If it looks correct, execute the three commands in the SUB file by giving the command:

SUBMIT TEST <CR>

With CP/M Plus, unlike earlier versions of CP/M, the batch file with the SUB extension can be on any drive.

As SUBMIT encounters each line in the SUB file, it will display the line on the console exactly as if you had typed it on the keyboard. Even the A> prompt will be shown. CP/M will then execute each command line in turn. Because the display moves so quickly, you may not have time to see your commands on the screen. Remember that you can use ^S to stop the display and then ^Q to start it again. If you want to terminate SUBMIT before it has finished, press ^C.

Our example showed only one simple use for SUBMIT. You will be able to use it for many more important applications. For example, suppose you want to obtain a printed listing of five different text files located on drive B. You can create a file called LIST.SUB on drive A that executes PIP five times. The file might look like this:

```
PIP  LST: = B:FILE1.TXT
PIP  LST: = B:FILE2.TXT
PIP  LST: = B:FILE3.TXT
PIP  LST: = B:FILE4.TXT
PIP  LST: = B:FILE5.TXT
```

Turn on your printer and give the command:

SUBMIT LIST <CR>

Then you can go out for coffee while the files are printing.

Automatic Execution on Startup   Each time you turn on your computer, CP/M Plus looks for a disk file named PROFILE.SUB. If it is present, CP/M directs SUBMIT to execute the commands that are present. In this way, the system can automatically perform various housekeeping tasks that are needed each time the computer is turned on. If the file PROFILE.SUB is not present, CP/M continues normal operation.

As with the previous example, you must create the PROFILE.SUB file with the system editor or with PIP. A good candidate for PROFILE. SUB is the command:

SETDEF A:, *

This command directs CP/M to look first on drive A for a transient program. If the program cannot be found on A, CP/M will look on the current drive. Be sure that PROFILE.SUB is located on disk A if you want CP/M to execute it at each cold start.

Batch Processing with Dummy Parameters   Another powerful feature of SUBMIT is the ability to interpret dummy parameters in the SUB file. A *dummy parameter* is a symbol that is replaced by the actual parameter at execution time. A dummy parameter in a SUB file is indicated by a dollar sign followed by a number, starting with 1. This allows slight variations in interpretation of the commands.

As an example, suppose we have a file called PRNT.SUB containing the line:

PIP LST: = FILE.TXT

The command:

SUBMIT PRNT

will send the file named FILE.TXT to the printer. However, suppose we change the submit file to:

PIP LST: = $1

That is, we replace the file name with the dummy name $1. Then if we give the command:

    SUBMIT PRNT FILE.TXT

the result will be the same as before. SUBMIT substitutes the second parameter FILE.TXT for the dummy parameter $1.

Our SUB file is now more versatile because of the dummy parameter. For example, we can print a file called SORT.BAS by giving the command:

    SUBMIT PRNT SORT.BAS <CR>

This time, SUBMIT issues the command:

    PIP LST: = SORT.BAS

because SUBMIT replaced the dummy parameter $1 by the second parameter SORT.BAS.

In the previous example we used a dummy parameter for a file name. However, dummy parameters can replace any set of characters, not just a file name. We could have included the drive name in the parameter as well as the file name. For example, the command:

    SUBMIT PRNT B:SORT.BAS

will print the file located on drive B.

Additional dummy parameters can be added as needed. They appear in order as $1, $2, $3, and so forth.

For example, suppose we change our SUB file to:

    PIP LST: = $1
    PIP LST: = $2
    PIP LST: = $3

so there are three dummy parameters. The corresponding command:

    SUBMIT PRNT FILE1 FILE2 FILE3

directs CP/M to execute SUBMIT. The first parameter tells SUBMIT to use the file PRNT.SUB. The remaining parameters are to be substituted for the corresponding dummy parameters $1, $2, and $3. Thus SUBMIT will generate the lines:

```
PIP  LST: = FILE1
PIP  LST: = FILE2
PIP  LST: = FILE3
```

A dollar sign is used in the SUB file to indicate a dummy parameter. However, you may sometimes need to use a dollar sign as a regular symbol in a command line. SUBMIT resolves this potential conflict of symbols in an interesting way. When a dollar sign is needed as a regular character in a SUB file, you must supply two dollar signs. The double dollar sign becomes a single dollar sign in the final command line presented to CP/M.

Sometimes it is necessary to include a control character in a command. However, it is not convenient to place a control character in a text file as the system is likely to interpret the character as a command and execute it. In particular, control-Z is always interpreted as an end-of-file indicator and control-C may be interpreted as a warm start. To resolve this problem, we indicate control characters in SUB files with the ^ symbol. That is, control-C is indicated by actually entering two characters—the ^ symbol and the C symbol. Similarly, control-Z is obtained by entering both the ^ symbol and the letter Z.

Input to an Executing Program   We have seen how SUBMIT can execute regular CP/M commands from a disk file as though the commands were entered directly from the keyboard. It is also possible to include a SUBMIT command as a line in another SUBMIT file. That is, one SUBMIT file can initiate the execution of another SUBMIT file.

All the commands we have considered so far are typed on the command line in response to the CP/M prompt. Sometimes, however, we need to give information to a program after it has begun execution. Suppose, for example, we run PIP without a parameter and then give a sequence of commands to PIP's asterisk prompt:

```
PIP
LST: = FILE1.TXT
LST: = FILE2.TXT
LST: = FILE3.TXT
```

```
LST: = FILE4.TXT
LST: = FILE5.TXT
```

The first line, containing the command PIP, is given in response to the CP/M prompt. The remaining lines, however, respond to the PIP prompt. They cannot simply be placed into a SUB file since they are input to PIP not to CP/M. Rather, they must be specially marked to tell SUBMIT that they are not commands to CP/M. The < symbol is placed at the beginning of the line for this purpose. Thus, a SUB file to perform the steps looks like this:

```
PIP
<LST: = FILE1.TXT
<LST: = FILE2.TXT
<LST: = FILE3.TXT
<LST: = FILE4.TXT
<LST: = FILE5.TXT
<
```

Notice that there is a final < symbol to terminate PIP.

DEVICE

Logical and Physical Devices   The peripherals such as the console, printer, and phone modem are attached to the computer through *ports*. Since the number and type of ports will vary from one computer to another, the assigned names for the ports will vary also. Each port, and, by extension, the corresponding peripheral attached to the port, is called a *physical device*. The software that drives a port refers to a *logical device*. CP/M incorporates software for the logical devices CON: (for console), LST: (for printer), and AUX: (for an auxiliary device such as a modem). Notice that we have already used CON: and LST: in PIP commands.

The name CON: is actually a shorthand way of referring to two separate sets of routines. These are the console input routines (CONIN:) and the console output routines (CONOUT:). The name AUX: also refers to auxiliary input (AUXIN:) and auxiliary output (AUXOUT:) routines. Both the console and auxiliary ports are *bidirectional;* that is, they can transfer both ways, output to the peripheral and input from the peripheral. By contrast, the printer is only an output port. Consequently, LST: refers to only one routine. Let us see how to use DEVICE.

Give the command:

DEVICE NAMES

to determine the physical device names incorporated into your CP/M computer. The result might be:

CRT 9600 IOS MODEM 300 IOS PRNTR 2400 OS CEN NONE O

This response shows four physical devices—CRT (console), MODEM, PRNTR (printer), and CEN (Centronics printer). Notice that a colon is not used at the end of these physical device names. The third item contains an I for input device, an O for output device, and an S for serial device. We can see that CRT and MODEM are both input and output serial devices. Both printers are output devices, but one is serial and the other is not. The number following the first three names specifies the serial transfer rate. The last device is not serial and so does not have an associated transfer rate. Any of these physical devices may be assigned to the five CP/M logical devices.

Let us next determine the current assignment. Give the command:

DEVICE VALUES

The result might be:

```
CONIN: = CRT
CONOUT: = CRT
AUXIN: = MODEM
AUXOUT: = MODEM
LST: = PRNTR
```

indicating that console input and output refer to CRT, auxiliary input and output refer to MODEM, and printer output goes to the serial printer. The logical device names in the left column of the list will always be the same. However, the physical device names in the right column will be different from one computer to the next. For example, a computer manufacturer might choose the name TERMNL for the console and DIABLO and CENTR for two printers, and there may be no MODEM.

If you execute DEVICE without a parameter, both the NAMES listing and the VALUES listing shown above are given. Then the program waits for your input. You can now change the current assignment or you can change the characteristics of the corresponding ports. Let us see how.

Some computers have only two ports—one for the console and one shared by both the printer and the modem. To use the modem, it is necessary to unplug the printer and then plug the modem into that port. You must then assign, or *map,* the logical AUX: device to the physical printer port. It may also be necessary to change the transfer rate. Let us consider just the reassignment first. The command might be:

        DEVICE AUX: = PRNTR

if the physical device MODEM is not shown in the listing of devices. Otherwise, the command is:

        DEVICE AUX: = MODEM

You may also have to set the transfer rate to the value required by the modem. This is likely to be either 300 or 1200. For example, to assign the AUX: port and set the transfer rate to 300, give the command:

        DEVICE AUX: = PRNTR[NOXON,300]

This command also disables X-ON protocol, the usual case. (If X-ON protocol is needed, use the option XON instead of NOXON.)

When you have finished with the modem and want to reset the port for the printer, check the original NAMES listing to determine the original printer speed. If you found it to be 2400, give the command:

        DEVICE LST: = PRNTR[NOXON,2400]

to set the port back to its original speed.

Sending Information to More Than One Device   Normally, one physical device will be assigned to each logical device. However, the

DEVICE command can map more than one physical device to each logical device. For example, the command:

    DEVICE CONOUT: = CRT,PRNTR

will send all console output simultaneously to the console screen and to the printer. (Remember, the physical device name may be different for your computer.) Return the mapping to its regular assignment with the command:

    DEVICE CONOUT: = CRT

It appears that, in the previous example, mapping the console output to both the console and the printer performs the same task as pressing ^P. However, there is a subtle difference in the way the mapping is accomplished. For example, ^P cannot be used to engage the printer when certain programs such as MBASIC are executing. By contrast, CONOUT: can be mapped to both the console and the printer before executing MBASIC. Then all console output will appear at both the console and printer.

If you find that you always need to issue the same DEVICE commands each time your computer is turned on, place these commands in your PROFILE.SUB file so they will be executed automatically.

SUMMARY

In this chapter, we have considered the most frequently used CP/M commands. We defined commands, parameters, and options, and discussed the difference between built-in commands and transient commands and extensions. You should now know how to use the built-in commands TYPE, USER, DIR, DIRSYS, RENAME, and ERASE; and the transient commands SETDEF, SHOW, SET, SUBMIT, and DEVICE.

A summary of these commands, as well as all the other CP/M Plus commands, is presented in reference form in Chapter 7.

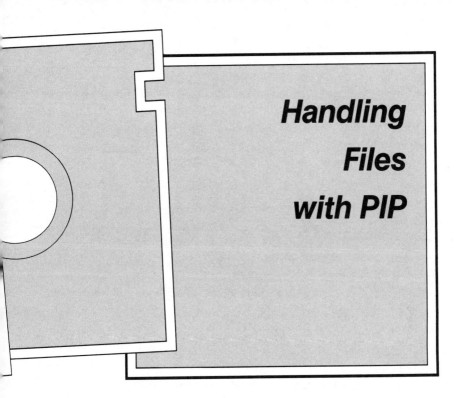

Handling
Files
with PIP

INTRODUCTION

PIP is a separate program that comes with the CP/M operating system. We have already studied some of the most useful PIP commands in earlier chapters. Because PIP is one of the most important utility programs, we will devote this entire chapter to learning more about it.

PIP is primarily a file transfer program. As its name suggests, (the letters PIP stand for Peripheral Interchange Program), PIP is used to transfer files from one device, such as a disk, to another, such as the console. However, it has many other features. Among other functions, PIP can:

- Copy a single file from one disk to another
- Copy a group of files from one disk to another
- Copy all files from one disk to another
- Create a file that is a duplicate of another file but has a different name
- Format text that is printed
- Reduce lines that are too long
- Print a group of files with just one command
- Join several files into a single file
- Extract a portion of a text file
- Translate a file to uppercase letters
- Translate a file to lowercase letters
- Reset the parity bit
- Add line numbers to a file
- Show a file on the screen during transfer
- Copy system files
- Copy files from one user area to another
- Copy files that have not been previously copied

Though you may need only a few of PIP's capabilities, it is important to know what features are available. Therefore, you are encouraged to read through this chapter completely, and then go back and study in detail the sections of specific interest to you or use the chapter for reference.

COPYING FILES

We will look first at PIP's most important function: copying files from disk to disk. As we have seen, PIP can copy a single file or a group of files. Let us begin with the single-file transfer.

Copying Single Files with Unambiguous Names

In the previous chapters, we learned to execute CP/M programs by typing the primary name on the command line. Usually, we have included parameters on the command line with PIP. For example, in Chapter 2 we gave the command:

```
PIP COPY.TXT = SAMPLE.TXT[V]
```

to make a copy of the program SAMPLE.TXT and name the new version COPY.TXT. This command contains three parameters—two file-name parameters and one option parameter. Notice that the new name comes first, and then the original name follows. Spaces on either side of the equals sign are optional. In this example both the original file and the new file reside on the same disk—the default, since the drive name was omitted from both file names.

The third parameter, V enclosed in square brackets, is an option parameter that stands for verify. It directs PIP to read the newly created file and compare it to the original file to ensure that it is correct. (PIP gives an error message if the copy is not correct.) You should always include the V option unless one of the devices is not a disk. Then you must not include the V option, since there is no way to verify the information. Whenever you use option parameters, there must never be a space before the left square bracket; that is, the bracket must immediately follow the file-name parameter. The right bracket, however, may be omitted.

When a file name refers to the default drive, you may omit the drive name, as illustrated in the previous example. There is no harm in including the drive name when you refer to the default drive, but it is not necessary. On the other hand, the drive name must be included when the file is not on the default drive. Consider, for example, the command:

```
PIP  B:COPY.TXT = C:SAMPLE.TXT[V]
```

This command copies the file SAMPLE.TXT from drive C to drive B and names the new copy COPY.TXT. Since both drives are specified, it does not matter what the default drive is.

In the previous two examples we have performed two tasks at once—copying a file and changing its name. If we want the new file to have the same name as the original file, we can simplify the command by omitting the copy name. In this case, we must give the drive name for the new file. For example, the command:

```
PIP  B: = C:SAMPLE.TXT[V]
```

copies the file SAMPLE.TXT from drive C to drive B. If the original file is on the default drive, we can omit the drive name. For example, if the default drive is C, the previous command could be shortened to:

    PIP B: = SAMPLE.TXT[V]

This is the most useful form for copying a single file.

Executing PIP without Parameters   PIP can be executed either with or without parameters. When you execute PIP by including parameters on the command line, PIP performs the requested task and then returns control to the CP/M operating system so you can give another command. However, when you execute PIP without a parameter, it displays its own prompt of * and awaits further commands. You can then give PIP a sequence of copy operations to perform. After each operation control returns to PIP rather than to CP/M. With this method the parameters you enter appear just as they would if you had given them on the command line with PIP. For example, you could execute the command in the previous section on two lines, thus:

    PIP <CR>
    B: = SAMPLE.TXT[V] <CR>

This method is more complicated when you want to give only one copy command. However, it is convenient when you want to give several PIP commands, since CP/M does not have to reload PIP after each step. In either case PIP performs its task in the same way.

The two methods of executing PIP respond differently if there is an error in your parameters. If PIP cannot find the original file you want to copy, it displays the message ERROR: FILE NOT FOUND and prints the name of the file it was looking for. If you included parameters with PIP on the command line, PIP then terminates its operation and returns to CP/M. However, if you initially executed PIP without a parameter, it does not terminate after displaying the error message. Rather, it gives the * prompt, indicating that it is ready to accept another command. PIP also responds differently to the Q and S options depending on how it was executed, as we will see later in this chapter.

After PIP displays the * prompt, you give a command. PIP performs the task and then gives the * prompt again. You can now enter another set of parameters for a second copy operation. At the end of this step, the * prompt appears again. You can continue in this way with an unlimited number of copying operations. For example, you can copy four files from drive C to drive B with the sequence:

```
PIP <CR>
B: = C:FILE1.TXT[V] <CR>
B: = C:FILE2.TXT[V] <CR>
B: = C:FILE3.TXT[V] <CR>
B: = C:FILE4.TXT[V] <CR>
```

When you are finished with PIP and want to return to CP/M, simply respond to the * prompt with a carriage return and the CP/M prompt will appear.

Rules for File Transfers   We will now present the rules for performing file transfers with PIP. To copy a file from one disk to another, use this form for the parameter:

```
d:copy = d:original[V]
```

In this example, d stands for the drive, copy for the new name of the copy file, and original for the name of the original file. The two drive names may refer to the same drive or to two different ones.

If you want the copy file to have the same name as the original file, you can omit the copy name. The abbreviated form is:

```
d: = d:original[V]
```

When only one name is given, PIP will assume that the name of the new file is the same as the original. When you use this form, the two drive names will usually be different. For example, the command:

```
B: = A:TEST.BAS[V]
```

will copy TEST.BAS from drive A to drive B.

Remember, the drive name may be omitted when it refers to the default drive. For example, the command:

```
B: = TEST.BAS[V]
```

copies the file TEST.BAS from the default drive to drive B.

Remember that you cannot have two files with the same name on the same disk. If you give the command:

B: = B:TEST.BAS[V]

PIP will make a copy of the file TEST.BAS. However, when PIP is done, it will erase the original file. No harm done, but no duplicate copy either. Later in this chapter, we will consider a use for this technique.

Let us look at some additional examples. Assume that the default drive is A and that the file FILE1.BAS is on drive A and the file PROGRAM.TXT is on drive B, When you execute PIP without a parameter, are the following PIP commands legal?

(1) A2 = B:PROGRAM.TXT
(2) B: = FILE1.BAS
(3) A:FILEREV.BAS = A:FILE1.BAS
(4) A:FILE1.TXT = FILE1.BAS
(5) B:FILE1.BAS = FILE1.BAS

All of the above PIP commands are proper. Notice that the command in example (2) is equivalent to:

B: = A:FILE1.BAS

because A is the default drive. Remember that you can omit the drive name when referring to the current drive if you give the file name.

The drive name A: could have been omitted from both file names in example (3). In (4) FILE1.TXT is not the same as FILE1.BAS; therefore, both files will exist on A after the operation. Example (5) could have been abbreviated to look like example (2).

The following commands are improper:

(1) = B:PROGRAM.TXT
(2) A: = FILE1.BAS
(3) B: = A:PROGRAM.TXT
(4) FILE1.BAS = FILE1.BAS
(5) B:FILE1.BAS = B:FILE1.BAS

Example (1) is incorrect because neither a drive name nor a file name is given for the first parameter. Example (2) is incorrect because both parameters refer to the same drive and file name since A is the default drive. The first two examples produce the PIP messages

ERROR: INVALID DESTINATION and ERROR: INVALID FORMAT. The third example is improper since it is trying to copy in the wrong direction—from A to B. The file is located on drive B rather than A. In this case PIP gives the message ERROR: FILE NOT FOUND—A: PROGRAM.TXT.

PIP will perform the operations indicated by examples 4 and 5. However, the result will be useless since the copy name is the same as the original and both refer to the same drive. Later we will consider adding an option parameter that will make operations (4) and (5) meaningful.

We have been copying individual files using unambiguous file names. Now let us see how to copy groups of files.

Copying Several Files with the Ambiguous ? and * Symbols

In the previous section we copied several files one at a time by first executing PIP without a parameter and then giving each copy command separately. There is another way to copy a group of files, as we saw in Chapter 2 when we copied all the files on disk A over to disk B with the command:

    PIP B: = A: * . * [V]

An ambiguous file name is one that contains the ? or * symbols. As we have seen, the question mark is like a wild card. It matches any single character, including a blank, in the given position. The asterisk indicates that PIP is to interpret the remainder of the field (the primary name or extension) as filled with question marks.

We can use an ambiguous file name as the second PIP parameter, the name of the original file. In this case the first parameter, the name of the copy file, must be simply a drive name such as A: or B:. For example, the command:

    PIP B: = SORT?. *

will copy all files that have SORT for the first four letters if the primary name has four or five letters—for example, SORT.BAS, SORT.BAK, SORT, and SORT2.BAS.

When an ambiguous file name is the second parameter, PIP will copy all files that match the name. In this case, PIP displays the expression COPYING - on the video screen, confirming that an ambiguous name was entered. Then, each time PIP locates a file that matches the ambiguous name, that file's name is displayed on the video screen and the file is copied. If PIP cannot find any file to match the ambiguous name, it displays the message ERROR: FILE NOT FOUND and repeats the ambiguous parameter.

For the next section we will need four files to practice with. We will now create them with PIP. Since we are going to need only the file names, not the contents of these files, we will trick CP/M into creating empty files, or files that contain no information.

If you have not established a file-search path, do so now. Give the command:

    A:SETDEF A:, *

Now you do not have to include the drive when you want to execute a program on disk A.

Make drive B current and execute PIP without a parameter. In response to the * prompt, give the command:

    FILE1.TRY = CON: <CR>

Be sure to include the colon after CON. CP/M places all the characters you type next into the new file. When you enter a ^Z to indicate the end of the file, CP/M places this character, too, into the file and then closes the file. Since we want an empty file, do not type any regular characters, just type a ^Z. You should then see the * prompt of PIP again. Continue in this way creating three additional files:

    FILE2.TRY = CON: <CR>
    FILE3.TRY = CON: <CR>
    FILE44.TRY = CON: <CR>

After you have created the fourth file, terminate PIP by giving just a carriage return. Check the directory with the command:

    DIR FILE*.TRY[FULL] <CR>

The listing will show these four new files. The number of bytes and number of blocks should be zero, since the files are empty and thus will not take up any disk space. (Of course, they do take directory space.)

We can copy the first three of these files from drive B to drive A with the following sequence of commands:

```
PIP <CR>
A: = B:FILE1.TRY <CR>
A: = B:FILE2.TRY <CR>
A: = B:FILE3.TRY <CR>
```

However, the command:

```
A: = B:FILE?.TRY <CR>
```

will perform the same transfer with just one command because of the ? matching character. And if drive B is the default, you can omit the B: drive name from the second parameter as well.

Try this command and watch it work. Notice that the file FILE44 .TRY is not copied because it does not match the ambiguous specification. If there had also been a file on drive B named FILES.TRY, it, too, would have been transferred by the ambiguous command.

The other matching character, the asterisk, is even more powerful. It will match any combination of characters in the remainder of its field, regardless of the length. Remember, CP/M expands the * symbol internally to a string of question marks. For example, if we wanted to transfer all four of the previous files with PIP, we could have given the command:

```
PIP A: = B:FILE*.TRY
```

As another example, assume drive B contains the files:

```
FILE1.TRY
FILE12.TRY
LETTER.TXT
CBASIC.INT
FILE1.BAK
```

The ambiguous name *.TRY will match the files:

```
FILE1.TRY
FILE12.TRY
```

and the name FILE1.* will match the files:

    FILE1.TRY
    FILE1.BAK

The expression *.* will match all the files in the directory.

We have now learned how to copy both a single file and a group of files using both ambiguous and unambiguous names. Next, we will learn ways to copy an entire disk.

Copying a Complete Disk

COPY and PIP   On many computers, a special utility program called COPY is available to duplicate an entire disk at one time. When this program is executed, the second disk will be an exact copy of the original, including the CP/M system tracks. This is usually the quickest way of copying a complete disk. However, COPY is not a standard CP/M program, so it is not available on all computers. Furthermore, COPY must be especially written for each different computer.

We have seen that CP/M stores information on the disk in units of 128 bytes, called sectors, which are collected into larger units known as blocks or groups. Larger files requiring more than one block are usually stored on a disk so the blocks are adjacent. However, after a file has been edited, the blocks of the new version may be scattered throughout the disk. Duplicating a disk with COPY will preserve this scattered condition because it makes an exact copy. By contrast, when PIP copies a file, it always places consecutive blocks as close together as possible, making the file more easily accessible.

Copying onto a Fresh Disk   As we discussed earlier, you should make backup copies of important disks. Let us consider several different methods for doing this.

Before you begin the copying operation, locate a disk and be sure it is properly formatted and set to RW if it is write protected (see Chapter 2). You can format a used disk, but it is not usually necessary.

If your computer has three or more disk drives, it is very easy to copy an entire disk. Place your system disk in drive A as usual. Insert a new disk in drive C and the disk you want to copy, which we will call the original disk, in drive B. Give the command:

PIP C: = B: * . *[V] <CR>

This command will copy all files except those marked as system files from drive B to drive C.

If you have only two drives, the copying process is more complicated. Let us consider two methods for duplicating disks with only two disk drives. The first method, which we will call *transferring through A,* is easier for copying one or two files. The second method, *disk swapping,* is easier when you must back up an entire disk. As long as you are inexperienced with CP/M, you should copy your files by transferring through A, because it is safer as well as simpler to use.

Copying Files by Transferring through Drive A   This method is safe but slow. Since it works only if disk A has enough space on it for all the backup files, you should use this method for backing up one or two files rather than an entire disk. Transferring through A is also suitable when drive A is a large floppy disk or a hard disk.

We begin with the system disk in drive A and the original disk to be backed up in drive B. The steps are as follows:

1. Copy the files from drive B to drive A using PIP.
2. Change to the new disk in drive B.
3. Copy the files from drive A to drive B using PIP.

The commands needed to copy a file by the transferring through A method look like this:

PIP A: = B:FILE.TXT[V]   (Copy from B to A)
(Place new disk in B.)
PIP B: = A:FILE.TXT[V]   (Copy from A to B)

Verify that the backup file is on the new disk in drive B by giving the command DIR B:. Then erase the extra copy of the files that exists on drive A. Include the A: parameter in the file names if A is not the default drive. For the previous example, the command is:

ERASE A:FILE.TXT

Copying Files by Disk Swapping   This second method of making a backup disk with only two disk drives transfers files directly from the original disk to the new disk. Therefore, it is more convenient than the previous method for transferring several files.

Begin by placing the regular system disk in drive A and the disk that will receive the new copies (the destination disk) in drive B.

Execute PIP without a parameter. CP/M will copy PIP into memory and execute it, and PIP will respond with its asterisk prompt. After the activity light in drive A has turned off, remove the system disk and put it into its envelope. Insert into drive A the original disk with the files to be copied.

It may seem surprising to suggest removing the system disk containing PIP. Remember, however, that when the program is running, a copy of PIP is in the computer's memory and so we no longer need the system disk. Of course, we want to change back to the system disk in drive A before we complete the operation of PIP. Therefore, *do not terminate PIP until you put the system disk back into drive A. Do not type a carriage return or a ^C in response to the * prompt once PIP has been activated.*

If you inadvertently terminate PIP after removing the system disk, CP/M may terminate normally with the regular prompt. Alternatively, CP/M may attempt to read a copy of itself from the system tracks of disk A. If the disk you have inserted into drive A contains a valid copy of CP/M on the system tracks, there will be no problem. On the other hand, if the disk in drive A does not contain CP/M or if there is no disk in drive A, CP/M will no longer respond to your commands. You will then have to put your regular system disk in A and reboot CP/M. Placing CP/M on the system tracks of all your disks is an effective safeguard when an accidental exit from PIP occurs.

Assuming you have not inadvertently terminated PIP, it is now in memory, waiting for a command. The disk containing the original files is in drive A, and the fresh disk that will receive a copy of the files is in drive B. If you want to copy the entire original disk, enter the expression:

    B: = A: * . * [V] <CR>

or, if the default drive is A, the shorter expression:

    B: = * . * [V] <CR>

As we have seen, the *.* expression matches all files listed in the directory for the given drive. These files are copied from drive A to drive B. If there are system files to be copied, you must include the R parameter to read these files. The command is then:

B: = *.*[VR] <CR>

If there are no system files, no harm is done by including the R parameter.

After the command is executed, you will have a copy of every file, with the same names as before, on the fresh disk. The * prompt indicates that PIP is ready for another command. *Do not type a carriage return or* ^C at this time. Before terminating PIP, remove the original disk from drive A and replace it with the system disk. Now that the system disk is back in place, you can safely terminate PIP by simply pressing the RETURN key. The CP/M system prompt will then appear.

If the system prompt does not appear, check that you have inserted the system disk in drive A. If you have inserted an incorrect disk or there is no disk, the system may not respond. Remove all disks and shut off the system, and then restart in the usual way. The new backup disk you just created should be all right.

A Third Technique If your disks are large enough so you can spare about 30K bytes, you might want to consider another method for copying files. Put a copy of the CP/M system on every disk by using COPYSYS and then put a copy of PIP on all your disks. With this arrangement you can place any disk in drive A and copy it directly to a new disk in drive B. However, you will lose about 30K bytes on each disk.

Aborting a Copy Operation If you want to terminate PIP prematurely while files are being copied—for example, if you notice a typographical error in your command—simply type a ^C.

CONCATENATING FILES

So far, we have been using PIP to make a copy of one or more files. In all cases, the copy has been identical to the original. In fact, we

included the V parameter to ensure that the copy was a faithful repro-
duction of the original. Sometimes we need to combine two or more
files into a new file. This procedure is called *concatenation*. Before we
go into the details of concatenation, let us consider the two types of
disk file.

Text and Nontext Files

Disk files may be divided into two categories—text files and nontext
(binary) files. Text files are prepared by the user and include such var-
ied items as letters, reports, and computer programs written in
BASIC, Pascal, and FORTRAN. As we saw in Chapter 3, text files are
written with ASCII characters—the letters; the digits; the special symbols such as $,%,&, and *; and certain control characters such as the
carriage return, the line feed, and the form feed. (Appendix D
presents the full set of ASCII characters.) CP/M uses the ^Z symbol to
indicate the end of the text in a text file; no text may extend beyond a
^Z. Consequently, ^Z cannot be used as a valid character within a
text file.

Binary files are different from text files in that they can contain
every possible combination of characters, including the ^Z character. Consequently, ^Z does not mark the end of a binary file. COM
files are binary files. PIP always assumes a binary file when making a
copy of any file so the copy is always correct. However, when concatenating files, PIP assumes it is working with text files.

Concatenating Text Files

The PIP character that indicates concatenation is the comma. This
is why you should not use a comma in a file name. A simple example
of concatenation is:

```
PIP BIG.TXT = PART1.TXT,PART2.TXT
```

This command creates the new file BIG.TXT by combining the two
files PART1.TXT and PART2.TXT. In this example all three files are on

the default drive, since no drive name is included with the file names. The two original files still exist unchanged. Of course, there must be room on the disk for the new file as well as the original files.

CP/M always marks the end of a text file with a ^Z symbol. After concatenation, the new file contains the text of the first file up to but not including its ^Z character, followed by the text of the second file. Thus, the information in the new file appears in the exact order of the file names to the right of the equals sign.

You can concatenate more than two files by including additional file names, each separated from the next by a comma. For example, the command:

```
PIP  BIGGER.TXT = PART1.TXT,PART2.TXT,PART3.TXT
```

joins three text files. Again, all files in this example are on the default drive.

If you want PIP to verify that the concatenation is correct, you must include the V parameter after *each* file name. In the previous example, the V symbol must be inserted in three places. The command:

```
PIP  BIGGER.TXT = PART1.TXT[V],PART2.TXT[V],PART3.TXT[V]
```

will concatenate three files and verify that all three parts have been correctly incorporated into the new file.

You can concatenate files from different disks by including drive names with the file name. For example, the command:

```
PIP  C:BIG.TXT = B:PART1.TXT[V],B:PART2.TXT[V],B:PART3.TXT[V]
```

combines three files from drive B into a new file on drive C and verifies that the copy is correct.

Sometimes it is necessary to append one or two files to the end of another file with the new file having the same name as one of the original files. For example, the command:

```
PIP  FIRST.TXT = FIRST.TXT,SECOND.TXT,THIRD.TXT
```

combines the files FIRST.TXT, SECOND.TXT, and THIRD.TXT into a temporary file. If the concatenation is successful, the original file FIRST.TXT is deleted, and the concatenated version is given the original name FIRST.TXT. Of course, the files SECOND.TXT and

THIRD.TXT still continue to exist after the concatenation, but the original FIRST.TXT is erased.

A practical hint: when concatenating files, first use the SHOW command to make sure that there is enough room on the disk for the resulting file.

Now let us see how to concatenate nontext files.

Concatenating Nontext (Binary) Files

When PIP encounters a ^Z character during a concatenation step, it normally assumes that it has found the end of the file. However, as we have seen, ^Z does not mark the end of a binary file. Consequently, there is a potential problem when PIP concatenates binary files because ^Z is a valid character.

Since the most common type of binary program is the COM file, PIP has been programmed to ignore any ^Z it finds in a COM file and continue copying to the actual end of a file. Therefore, you can confidently concatenate COM files, although this is not very common. On the other hand, binary files with extensions other than COM will be incorrectly concatenated if they contain a ^Z character.

The way to solve this concatenation problem is to add the O option whenever you use PIP to concatenate binary files other than COM files. (The letter O stands for *object file,* another name for a binary file.) You do not need to use the O option when concatenating COM files, though it will do no harm. However, you must *not* use the O parameter when concatenating text files, or they will be incorrectly joined. It is not necessary to give the O parameter when you simply *copy* binary files, even if the file type is not COM. PIP always copies the entire file.

Inserting Characters During Concatenation

It is possible to insert characters from the console during a concatenation step. For example, suppose you give the command:

```
PIP NEW = FILE1,CON:,FILE2,CON:,FILE3
```

This command will direct PIP to create the file NEW beginning with the existing file FILE1. CON: tells PIP to then read any characters you enter from the keyboard and place them in the new file. Remember to use both <CR> and <LF> at the end of each line you enter from the keyboard. When you signal the end of the keyboard entry with a ^Z, PIP copies FILE2. PIP then reads characters from the keyboard until you type another ^Z. Finally, PIP copies FILE3. The characters you enter from the keyboard are displayed on the video screen. Be sure to enter a line feed after each carriage return and remember that you cannot correct typing errors with PIP.

Now let us see how to send disk files to a peripheral device such as the console or printer.

TRANSFERRING A DISK FILE TO A PERIPHERAL DEVICE

PIP provides general-purpose transfer capabilities that allow a file to be copied not only from disk to disk, but also between various devices such as the console, printer, and phone modem. Let us now consider this mode of transfer. We begin with transfer from the console.

Creating a File

It is possible to transfer information from the console keyboard to a disk file. In effect, this creates a new file. In Chapter 2, we performed this operation with the command:

    A:PIP SAMPLE.TXT = CON:

(If you did not create this file on drive B in Chapter 2, please refer back to that chapter and do so now. We will work with this file in the following section.)

The first parameter of this command, SAMPLE.TXT, is the name of the newly created disk file. The second parameter, CON:, refers not to a disk file but to the console keyboard. The colon at the end of the word CON enables PIP to distinguish a peripheral device name from a disk file of the same name. If the colon were omitted, the command would direct PIP to copy the disk file named CON.

When you give this command, PIP reads each character typed at the keyboard and enters it into the disk file named SAMPLE.TXT. A ^Z terminates the operation.

This PIP command is not really very useful, since it is easier to create a file with the system editor. However, it demonstrates how PIP transfers information to a file from the console.

Displaying a Disk File on the Screen

In the previous section, we saw how to create a disk file from characters entered from the console keyboard. We can reverse the process simply by reversing the parameters. The command:

    PIP CON: = SAMPLE.TXT

will display the disk file SAMPLE.TXT on the video screen of the console. (If you did not set up a search path with SETDEF, you will have to insert the drive name A: at the beginning of the PIP command.) The action is diagrammed in Figure 4.1.

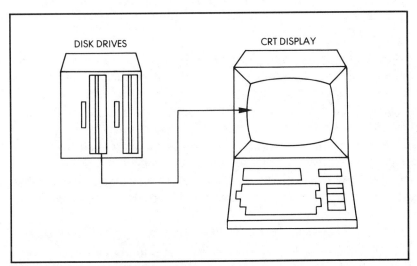

Figure 4.1 – PIP CON: = SAMPLE.TXT

This command may not appear to be very useful since we can perform the same operation with the built-in command:

TYPE SAMPLE.TXT

However, several PIP option parameters let you alter a file when it is copied to another disk or transferred to the screen or other peripheral.

Echoing Characters with the E Option   When PIP makes a copy of a disk file, no indication of progress is given on the video screen. Sometimes, however, you might find it helpful to see what is happening. If you use the E option, PIP displays (echoes) each character on the video screen during the copying. (*Echo* is the name used to describe the displaying of text during an operation.) Note, however, that the text is displayed too rapidly for you to read it line by line. Rather, E gives you a general idea of what is happening. You use the E parameter only with text files; it must not be used with nontext files, such as COM files.

Try out the E parameter with the short program we made using PIP. Give the command:

PIP SAMPLE.BAK = SAMPLE.TXT[E] <CR>

This will create a duplicate file and echo it on the screen during the copy operation.

Adding Line Numbers   Sometimes you may want to number the lines in a file. For example, it may be helpful to number the lines of a document you are preparing for a revision. Also, BASIC programs require line numbers. PIP can add a number to each line of a file during transfer. There are two variations of this parameter. The N option by itself adds line numbers that begin with 1 and are incremented by one. Blank spaces (called *leading* blanks) precede the number to fill out the field to six positions. A colon and a blank are appended at the end of the number. Thus, eight additional positions are added to the beginning of each line.

The parameter N2 produces line numbers in the form required by BASIC programs. With this version the number field is filled out with zeros rather than blanks, the colon is omitted, and the final (or *trailing*) blank is replaced by a tab character. This form adds seven characters to each line.

Try out both the N options by displaying the test file on the console with the commands:

```
PIP <CR>
CON: = SAMPLE.TXT[N] <CR>
CON: = SAMPLE.TXT[N2] <CR>
```

Changing Upper and Lower Case The L and U parameters can change the case of the letters A through Z. Adding the letter L changes all uppercase letters to lower case. The U option changes all lowercase letters to upper. Other characters are unaffected. To see the operation, try these commands:

```
PIP <CR>
CON: = SAMPLE.TXT[U] <CR>
CON: = SAMPLE.TXT[L] <CR>
```

Copying a Portion of a File

Sometimes you want to copy or display only a portion of a text file. Or perhaps you lost part of a long file listing either by accident (a power failure) or because of a printer problem (no more paper or other mechanical problems). You will want to restart your listing where it was interrupted, rather than list the entire file all over again. PIP provides an option for listing and transferring a portion of a file.

You can copy portions of a text file by specifying strings of characters where PIP is to start and stop. (A *string* is a sequence of characters. It may be a whole word or one or more characters in a row, such as part of a word.) Use the S parameter to specify a starting string (that is, where PIP should start copying), and the Q parameter to specify a quitting string (that is, where PIP should stop copying). End each string with ^Z. PIP will automatically search for the first occurrence of each string of characters and copy the text from the starting through the stopping string.

Here is an example that copies part of the file SAMPLE.TXT into a new file, named NEWSAMP.TXT:

```
PIP
NEWSAMP.TXT = SAMPLE.TXT[Qsecond ^Z]
```

This PIP operation starts copying at the beginning of the file and stops when it encounters the string second. Note that the string second is written in lowercase letters, and that you executed PIP in two lines, not as a one-line command. If you execute PIP without a parameter, and then type a PIP expression, CP/M will search for a string that looks exactly the way you typed it. In other words, if the file contains SECOND in uppercase letters, you would receive a message that CP/M had not found the quitting string. By contrast, if you execute PIP on a single line, CP/M will always translate your strings to upper case. If you had typed:

```
PIP  NEWSAMP.TXT = SAMPLE.TXT[Qsecond ^Z]
```

CP/M would automatically translate the string second to SECOND and so successfully locate the quitting string SECOND.

Here is another example using both the S and the Q parameters:

```
PIP
EXTRA.TXT = SAMPLE.TXT[Stext ^ZQsecond ^Z]
```

This PIP operation starts copying SAMPLE.TXT when it finds the string text and stops copying when it finds the string second. The file EXTRA.TXT will contain the portion of the file between the strings text and second, including both strings. Note that we executed PIP on two lines in order to preserve lowercase characters in the strings.

Printing a File with PIP

We have seen that there are several possible ways to obtain a printed listing of a text file. The simplest method, which we discussed in Chapters 2 and 3, is to engage the printer with ^P and then give the TYPE command. Another way is to use PIP. The operation is similar to the one we used to display a file on the console, with a major difference. PIP can interact with the console, through the parameter CON:, as both an input and an output device. By contrast, the printer (LST:) is only an output device. That is, a file cannot be transferred *from* the LST: device. The command:

PIP LST: = SAMPLE.TXT

sends the disk file SAMPLE.TXT to the printer. The action is diagrammed in Figure 4.2.

Later in this chapter, we will consider option parameters that can enhance the LST: command. Of course, all the regular PIP features can apply when you use PIP to print a file. Several files can be concatenated and printed with a single command. For example, the command:

PIP LST: = FILE1,FILE2,FILE3

will print the three files FILE1, FILE2, and FILE3.

An alternative printer device name PRN: allows for a variation in printing with PIP. When you use LST: to print a text file, the file is printed literally, as you entered it. When you use the PRN: device name, there is additional processing of the text. Each line is numbered sequentially, the ASCII tab character is expanded to eight

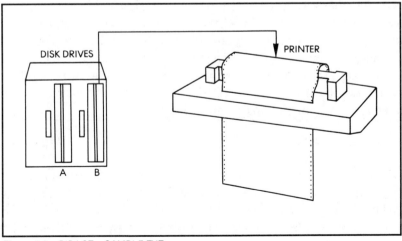

Figure 4.2 – PIP LST: = SAMPLE.TXT

columns, and the page-eject (form-feed) character is inserted every 60 lines. (These features are explained later in this chapter.) To see how this works, give the command:

    PIP PRN: = SAMPLE.TXT <CR>

LST: can perform the same operations if we include option parameters (see Chapter 7).

Making Backup Copies of Altered Files

It is important that you make frequent backup copies of important disk files whenever they are changed. We learned earlier in this chapter how to make copies of floppy disks using PIP. However, if you use a large hard disk, the situation is very different. It is not possible to copy the entire hard disk frequently if you must make the backup copy to a floppy disk. Of course, it is not necessary to copy the entire disk, only those files that have been changed since the last backup copy was made. PIP contains an option parameter to make this task easier.

We have seen that the attributes read only or read/write and system or directory are encoded in the directory with the file name. Another attribute encoded with the file name, the *archive* flag, indicates whether a file has been altered since the last archival copy operation. Each time a file is altered, the archive flag is automatically reset to indicate that the file has been changed. When a file is copied with the A (for archive) option, PIP changes the archive flag of the original to indicate that a backup copy has been made. Thus, at the end of each day you can copy all changed text files from your hard disk to a floppy with the ambiguous command:

    PIP B: = A: * .TXT[AV]

PIP will copy only those files that have been altered since the last copy operation and will then set the archive flag of these files so they will not be copied the next time.

The current state of the archive attribute can be determined with the FULL or RW option of DIR. The expression Arcv appears in the attribute column if the option is set—that is, if the file has been backed up. Otherwise, no entry appears in this column.

SETTING UP A NEW USER AREA

As we saw in Chapter 3, each disk can be logically partitioned into as many as 16 separate user areas. The advantage of separate user areas, the isolation of files, is also a disadvantage. Programs in one user area are not normally accessible to someone working in another area with one exception: system files located in user area 0 are accessible to all user areas. Furthermore, you should only partition a disk into several user areas if it is very large   for example, a double sided 8-inch floppy or a hard disk.

We learned in Chapter 3 how to determine the active user areas by executing SHOW with the [USERS] option and how to determine what files are associated with each user area by executing DIR with the [USER] option. Now let us see how to copy files from one user area to another.

Before partitioning a disk into several user areas, you should set the system attribute of all transient programs in user area 0. If this has not already been done, go to drive A and give the command:

    SET *.COM[SYS RO] <CR>

to set all COM files to both system and read-only status, making them accessible to all user areas.

To copy files from your current user area to another user area and vice versa, you use PIP with the G option. Before you begin a copy operation, determine the total size of the files on the source disk by executing DIR with the [SIZE] option. Then execute SHOW to ensure that there is sufficient space remaining on the destination disk. (Refer to Chapter 3 if you need to review these commands.)

Now let us consider a command to copy all BASIC programs from user area 0 on drive B to user area 2 on drive A. Be sure you are located in user area 0 on drive B. Give the command:

    A:PIP A:[G2] = *.BAS[V] <CR>

We have seen that several options can be placed after the source parameter, the second file name. However, in this example we use the G option after the destination parameter, the first file name. This is the only PIP option that can appear after the first file-name parameter.

An alternative method is available when user area 2 on drive A is current and PIP has been set to a system file. The command is:

PIP A: = B: * .BAS[G0 V]

(PIP options can be run together or separated with a space.) For either method, PIP will display each file name on the console as it is being copied because the ambiguous symbol * is included in the name.

Figure 4.3 diagrams the paths PIP follows in copying files from user areas on one disk to a user area on another disk. Suppose you are currently working in user area 1 of disk A but you need copies of files from drives B and C. One path shows PIP copying a file from your own user number of drive C. The command is:

PIP COPY1 = C:ORIG1[V]

Though the other two paths may look more direct òn the diagram,

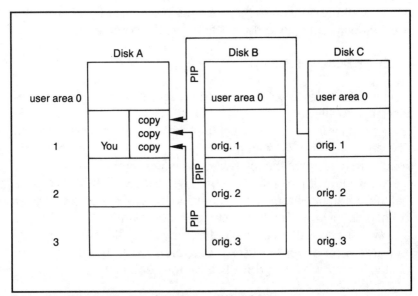

Figure 4.3 – Copying Files from Other Disks and User Areas

they require more complicated commands since the files are in different user areas. The commands are:

    PIP COPY2 = B:ORIG2[G2 V]
    PIP COPY3 = B:ORIG3[G3 V]

COPYING READ-ONLY AND SYSTEM FILES

PIP will not normally overwrite—in effect, delete—a file that has the read-only attribute set. For example, suppose that you give the command:

    PIP B:COPY = ORIG

but a read-only file named COPY already exists on drive B. PIP responds with the question:

    DESTINATION FILE IS R/O, DELETE (Y/N)?

If the existing file named COPY did not have the RO attribute, PIP would have automatically deleted the original COPY and replaced it with the new COPY. Because of the RO attribute, PIP displays the message that the file named COPY is read only and asks if you want to delete the original version of COPY. If you reply Y (yes), PIP will delete the old COPY and replace it with the new COPY. (Note that with a simple Y or N answer you do not press RETURN.) If you answer N for no, PIP terminates without performing the copy operation, and the original version of COPY is not deleted. PIP displays the message:

    * * NOT DELETED * *

If you want to override this step of a message and response when a file is read only, you can use the W parameter. PIP will then ignore the RO attribute, delete the file, and proceed with the operation. When concatenating several files, you need to give the W parameter only once at the end of the PIP expression. For example:

    PIP WHOLE.TXT = PART1.TXT,PART2.TXT,PART3.TXT[W]

If the original file has the system attribute, then PIP cannot find it in the disk directory. For example, if PIP.COM is a system file on disk A and you want to make a copy on disk B, the command:

    PIP B: = A:PIP.COM

will not work. You must give the R parameter to copy a system file. For example:

    PIP B: = A:PIP.COM [R]

Therefore, when you want to copy a system file, you must use the R option so PIP can locate the file. Furthermore, if the COPY file exists as a system file, PIP will delete it and then make the new version a system file.

If several files are being concatenated, the R parameter must be given for each one. For example, the command:

    PIP WHOLE.TXT = PART1.TXT[R],PART2.TXT[R],PART3.TXT[RW]

will concatenate the three system files PART1.TXT, PART2.TXT, and PART3.TXT into a new file named WHOLE.TXT. If a file named WHOLE.TXT already exists and is write protected, PIP will automatically erase it because the W parameter is also included.

ZEROING THE PARITY BIT

The ASCII character set only uses seven bits. Consequently, the remaining bit of each byte, called the *parity bit,* can be used as an error check. However, sometimes this bit is used for other purposes. For example, WordStar in the document mode sets the parity bit to indicate spacing for justification. On the other hand, Microsoft BASIC requires the parity bit to be reset. Thus, if a BASIC program is edited with the document mode of WordStar, the parity bit will be set for many of the characters and the BASIC program can no longer be used. When this happens, use the Z option of PIP to restore the BASIC program to its original form by zeroing the parity bit. For example, the command:

    PIP SORT.BAS = SORT.BAS[VZ]

will make the program SORT.BAS usable again. Notice that in this example both the original file and the new file have the same name. Do not use ambiguous characters in this case or you may lose your file. The Z parameter is not needed for transfer to ASCII devices such as CON: and LST: and it must *not* be used for copying binary files or WordStar files.

USING OPTION PARAMETERS WITH PIP

We have been able to modify the operation of PIP by including option parameters such as V and E enclosed in square brackets at the end of the PIP command. When you include more than one parameter in a PIP expression, the parameters can be given in any order and may be separated by spaces. The D, G, P, and T options require a number immediately following. The Q and S parameters need a string of characters and ^Z.

Now let us look at some examples of PIP expressions using option parameters:

    PIP LST: = SAMPLE.TXT [NT8P60]

This expression sends the file SAMPLE.TXT to the printer (LST:), adds line numbers (N), expands tabs to every eighth character column (T8), and inserts form feeds every 60 lines (P60). If you assign PRN: as the listing device, these are the default parameters. Thus, you could obtain the same result by rewriting the above example as:

    PIP PRN: = SAMPLE.TXT

Here is another example of PIP options:

    PIP LST: = PROG.ASM[NT8U]

This expression sends PROG.ASM to the printer with line numbers (N), tabs expanded to every eighth column (T8), and lowercase characters translated to upper case (U).

In this chapter, we have explored some of the PIP options. Even though you will generally use only a few of the many options available, it is important to be aware of them in case you need them. The PIP options are summarized in Chapter 7.

SUMMARY

PIP is a powerful general-purpose file-transfer program. Though it is most frequently used for simple disk-to-disk transfers, it can do much more. For example, PIP can:

- Verify that the new copy is correct
- Transfer files between devices and disks
- Transfer several files at once
- Alter certain properties of a file
- Join several files into a new file
- Extract a portion of a file
- Copy files from one user area to another
- Copy files that have been altered.

This chapter discussed the most common options used with PIP. A working knowledge of the important capabilities of this program is a definite advantage to every CP/M user.

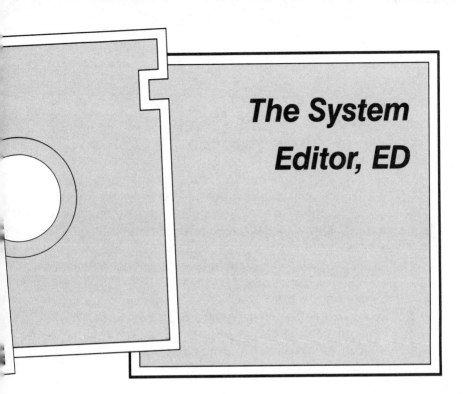

The System
Editor, ED

INTRODUCTION

In Chapter 2 we used the CP/M program PIP to create a very short text file. This is not a convenient way to create larger files since we cannot correct typing errors during entry or alter the resulting file with PIP. Consequently, CP/M includes an editor program that can create and alter disk files.

If you use a computer for writing computer programs or for letters and reports, you will need to use an editor. There are several editor programs that may come with your computer or that you can purchase separately. Some editors are easy to learn but not very sophisticated, whereas other editors are very powerful but may be difficult to master.

ED, the editor included with CP/M, is easy to learn compared to most editors, but it is quite cumbersome and inefficient to use. ED is reasonably satisfactory for writing line by line, as in computer programs, but it is less convenient for composing and altering general text that is organized into paragraphs. If ED is the only editor provided with your computer, you should seriously consider purchasing a more powerful program.

In this chapter we will learn to use the CP/M system editor, ED. If you will always be using a different editor with your computer, you can skip on to the next chapter.

Before we learn the specific ED commands, let us consider what a text editor is and how it is used.

WHAT IS A TEXT EDITOR?

If you want to write a computer program, a business letter, or a manuscript, you need to create a text file that is saved on disk. Furthermore, after you have created such a file, you may want to make alterations or additions to it. A text editor is used for both the creation and the alteration of text files.

When you create a document with an editor, you type the text as you would with a typewriter. The resulting disk file can be displayed on the video screen or sent to the printer by the methods we discussed in earlier chapters. When a text editor alters an existing file, it does not actually change the original copy. Rather, it creates a new disk file that incorporates the desired changes. The original file is then saved as a backup copy.

The real power of the editor is apparent when you want to make changes to the document. An editor should allow you to move easily from place to place in the document and to make changes by typing new text directly over the original or by deleting and inserting new characters. The editor should be able to locate a selected passage in

the text so you can readily make changes. An editor will also let you insert text from another file. ED provides all of these features.

Sophisticated editors let you easily move the cursor anywhere on the screen to make changes. Unfortunately, ED does not provide this capability.

A word processor is a special type of editor that can not only create and alter text files but can also format the resulting text for the printer. Word processor capabilities include underlining, justifying margins, subscripting, superscripting, and creating boldface type. ED is not designed for these operations.

Let us begin by learning how ED operates. Then we will see how to use the specific commands.

HOW ED OPERATES

The CP/M text editor resides on the system disk under the name ED.COM. If you have a large hard disk, you can use it as the system disk and perform all the editing operations on it too. However, if you have a floppy disk system with limited storage space, you must be more careful. In this chapter we will assume you are using floppy disks.

You execute the program by typing the primary name ED followed by the name of the file you want to create or alter. For example, the command:

ED SAMPLE.TXT

executes ED and instructs it to look for a file named SAMPLE.TXT on the current drive. If the file can be located, ED prepares to edit it. If no such file exists, ED will create a new one.

You can execute ED with two parameters. In this case the first parameter indicates the original file, and the second parameter refers to the new file. If you execute ED without parameters, it will automatically ask for the first and second parameters. If only one file name is desired, as is usually the case, simply give a carriage return when the second parameter is requested.

When you create a new disk file with ED, all the text you type is initially placed into a region of memory known as the *edit buffer*. At the completion of the editing step, ED makes a file that is a copy of the edit buffer.

The edit buffer is a block of memory in the TPA (transient program area) where the editing is actually done. The entire original file can be loaded into the buffer if it will fit. If the file is too large, however, only a portion of it is copied into the buffer. When this portion has been edited, it is written to a new file. Additional text is then copied into the edit buffer from the original file. In this way you can edit a long file.

When altering an existing file, an editor does not actually change the original version but creates a second file that contains the desired changes. If you entered only one parameter, ED will give the original name to the new version of the file. It will not delete the original file but will change its file-name extension to BAK. In the example of SAMPLE.TXT the original file, also called the *source file,* will be renamed to SAMPLE.BAK at the end of the editing session.

When there is enough room on the disk, both the new file and the original file will reside on the disk at the conclusion of the editing session. However, if the file to be edited is very large or there is a limited amount of space on the disk, there will not be room for both files. In this case you must place the new file on another disk.

When you want to edit a file and place the edited file on another disk, you give two parameters to the ED command. For example, when drive B is current, the command:

    A:ED SAMPLE.TXT A:

directs ED to look for the original file on drive B, the first parameter, and to place the edited version of the file on drive A, the second parameter. If the second parameter consists of only a drive name, ED automatically fills out the second parameter with the file name of the first parameter. In this example the file type of the original file will not be changed since the two parameters refer to different drives. Of course, you can give a different file name for the second parameter.

Altering an existing disk file is more complicated than creating a new file. To accept any changes or additions, your file must be in the edit buffer. Many text editors automatically copy the original file into the edit buffer so you can make the desired alterations. However, once you have executed the ED program, you must give a specific command to copy the original file into the edit buffer. Then you alter the version in the edit buffer by giving the appropriate commands. Finally, you create a new disk file from the edit buffer. Thus, text moves from the original file to the edit buffer and then to the new disk file. The relationship of the edit buffer to the disk files and the console is shown in Figure 5.1.

In previous chapters we learned how to edit the command line with control characters. Three of these commands can be used with either the insert or the command mode of ED— ^H, ^X, and ^U.

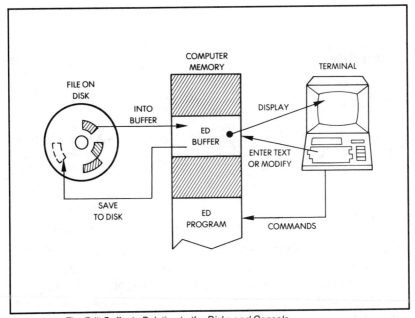

Figure 5.1 – The Edit Buffer in Relation to the Disks and Console

The cursor is moved to the left with ^H, and the current line is canceled with either ^X or ^U. You can give the other CP/M Plus line-editing commands when ED is in command mode.

The regular ED commands are not control characters but simply letters of the alphabet. That is, you type the letter without holding down the control key. For most commands either uppercase or lowercase letters may be used. (We will see the exceptions later in this chapter.) The letter usually suggests the nature of the operation—for example, A for append and W for write.

If you want to execute a command more than once, you can precede the letter by a parameter indicating how many times it is to be repeated. If you omit the parameter, ED usually performs the command once. You use the number symbol (#) as a parameter when you want to repeat the command as many times as possible. (# is ED's shorthand for 65,535.) As we will see, a parameter of zero sometimes has special meaning. Always give a carriage return at the end of the command line, even when there is only one character.

To better understand how ED operates, we are now going to create and alter a simple file. We will discuss the various editing commands in more detail in later sections.

USING ED

Creating a File

Place the system disk containing ED.COM in drive A and a working disk in drive B. (Make sure this disk does not already contain files named SAMPLE.TXT and SAMPLE.BAK.) Make drive B current and give the command:

    A:ED SAMPLE.TXT

If you have established a search path with SETDEF as described in Chapter 3, you can omit the drive name from the ED command.

ED will display the message NEW FILE, indicating that it is adding a new file name to the disk directory. If this message appears when you want to alter an existing file, it means that ED could not locate the requested file. Perhaps you misspelled the name, or perhaps you are on the wrong drive. In such a case you would return to CP/M by entering the Q command and giving ED the proper command. Various error messages you might receive as you work with ED are listed near the end of this chapter.

ED has two separate modes of operation—command mode and insert mode. As the names imply, you give commands to ED in command mode and add new text in insert mode. ED begins in command mode, as indicated by a colon followed by an asterisk.

Each time ED is started up, the edit buffer is empty. Therefore, the first thing you must do is copy all or part of the original file into the edit buffer. If the file is very short, it can be copied into the buffer all at once. However, if the file is large, the text must be passed through the edit buffer section by section. This operation is known as *paging* a file through the edit buffer. Let us consider the commands that transfer text through the edit buffer.

After you execute ED, a prompt of:

: *

should be on the video screen. Whenever the cursor is next to the asterisk, ED is in the command mode ready for your next command. Give the command:

i <CR>

ED will respond by moving down to the next line, which is numbered 1: The I command puts you in insert mode and lets you insert text into the buffer. We will look at this command in more detail later in the chapter. For now we will simply use it to create a file.

At the cursor on line 1, enter the following text:

This is the first line of my file SAMPLE.TXT. <CR>

ED will move down to the next line, numbered 2: Enter:

This is the second line. <CR>
This is the third line. <CR>
This is the fourth line. <CR>

At the fifth line enter ^Z. This will mark the end of your file. It takes you out of the edit buffer and returns you to command mode. Now give the command:

E <CR>

to end the edit and write the text from the buffer to your disk file. The B> prompt shows that you are back in CP/M.

Next we will see how to alter an existing file.

Altering a File

To return to ED, with drive B current give the command:

A: ED SAMPLE.TXT

Notice that this time you do not see the message NEW FILE. At the cursor give the command:

#A <CR>

to copy (append) as many lines as possible from the source file into the edit buffer. Since your source file contains only four lines, you could accomplish the same thing with the command 4A. This is diagrammed in Figure 5.2.

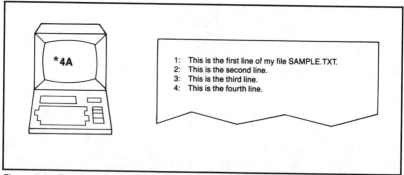

1:   This is the first line of my file SAMPLE.TXT.
2:   This is the second line.
3:   This is the third line.
4:   This is the fourth line.

Figure 5.2 – Text is Appended to the Buffer with the A Command.

Very large files that do not entirely fit into the edit buffer are edited in steps. You first copy some lines into memory with the A command. After editing, you write these lines to the new file with the W command. Additional lines are read into the edit buffer with another A command, and so forth. In this way you can edit a large file with a series of A and W commands. The command 0A is useful for this because it copies lines from the source file until the buffer is about half full.

The cursor at line 1 indicates you are now in the edit buffer and can begin editing your text. You'll notice, however, that your text doesn't appear on the screen. To display your text, give the command:

    #T <CR>

Alternatively, you could enter T alone to display one line, or T with a number preceding it for a specific number of lines.

As a simple example of a text alteration, we will add two more lines to the file. Give the command:

    -B <CR>

This will move the cursor to the end of the file. Next give the command:

    i <CR>

You will see that you are now at line 5, and can insert new text. Enter:

    This is the fifth line. <CR>
    This is the sixth line. <CR>
    ^Z

After you finish editing the file, give the E command to end the edit. ED automatically writes any remaining lines from the edit buffer to the new file, copies unchanged any remaining lines of the original file to the new file, and then returns to CP/M. To see how this works, give the E command followed by <CR>. Next give the command:

    DIR S*.*[FULL] <CR>

to see that files named SAMPLE.TXT and SAMPLE.BAK are both present. (If you have not established a search path, you must add the A: drive name to DIR.)

Now that we have learned how to create a file and to transfer text from the source file to the edit buffer and then to the new file, let us consider the character pointer and how to move it.

COMMANDS FOR MANIPULATING THE CHARACTER POINTER

ED can alter information in the edit buffer by deleting or inserting single characters or complete lines. To do this, you must specify exactly where you want the alterations to occur by using the *character pointer* (sometimes abbreviated CP), an invisible marker that can be moved through the edit buffer. Note that the character pointer is not the same as the video cursor. ED commands that delete or insert information refer to this pointer.

Unfortunately, most of the movements of the pointer through the text are not automatically displayed on the screen. To see exactly where you are after each move, you must give the T command. For example, once you have executed ED, give the following commands:

```
#A <CR>
#T <CR>
3C <CR>
```

Although the pointer has moved three characters to the right in the first line, the change doesn't show on the screen. Now type:

```
T <CR>
```

ED now displays the line beginning at the position of the pointer.

The pointer can be positioned at the beginning of the buffer, between any two characters of the text, or at the end of the edit buffer. ED initially sets the pointer to the beginning of the buffer. You can always return the pointer to the beginning of the buffer by issuing the B command (see Figure 5.3). The command may be given in either upper or lower case. The command -B moves the pointer to the end of the buffer.

The C command moves the pointer one or more characters, and the L command moves it one or more lines. Remember that the

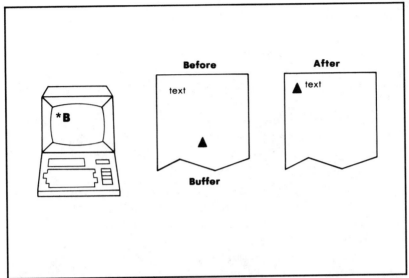

Figure 5.3 – The B Command Moves the Pointer to the Beginning of the Buffer.

carriage return and line feed at the end of the line each count as one character. A number preceding either command indicates the number of characters or lines the pointer is to move. For example, the command 5L moves the pointer ahead (toward the end of the buffer) by five lines. A negative parameter moves the pointer back toward the beginning of the buffer. (Use the hyphen on your keyboard for the negative sign.) For example, a command of -7C moves the pointer backward seven characters. This is the usual interpretation of the minus sign in CP/M commands. Notice that in the previous example the minus sign in -B has the opposite effect.

Giving the L and C commands without a parameter moves the pointer one line or character. As with the A and W commands, a parameter of # moves the pointer the maximum number of characters or lines. This will be the end of the buffer. It will also be the end of the file except for a large file. The command 0L moves the pointer to the beginning of the current line.

An interesting variation on the L command occurs when you give only the parameter itself. For example, a command of 6 moves the pointer ahead six lines and then displays the sixth line on the console. If you give a carriage return by itself, ED moves the pointer to the next line and displays that line. A parameter of just a minus sign moves the pointer back one line and displays that line.

Searching for a String of Characters

In addition to moving the character pointer a fixed number of characters or lines at a time, you can move the pointer to a particular string of characters with the F and N commands. Let us consider F first.

The F (for find) command locates the requested string in the edit buffer and places the pointer immediately *after* the string. The simplest form of the command is fstring, where string stands for the characters you want to find.

You must be aware of a few complications when you use the F command. First, if there are *any* lowercase letters in the string, you must enter the letter f in lower case. Otherwise, ED will raise all lowercase letters in the string to upper case before performing the search and won't find the string. This problem is not unique with the F command. Though ED commands can generally be given in either uppercase or lowercase letters, they must be in lower case whenever a following string of characters contains lowercase letters.

A second problem can occur because the F command can only move the pointer forward. Thus, ED searches for the next occurrence of the string starting at the character pointer. If the string you need is located between the beginning of the buffer and the pointer, the F command will not find it. The solution is to reset the pointer to the beginning of the buffer using the B command before you give the F command.

If you are going to give additional commands after the end of the string, you must include ^Z at the end of the string.

Let us look at an example of how the F command works. Execute ED for the file SAMPLE.TXT and type:

    fline

ED will locate the next occurrence of the string line after the position of the character pointer. The pointer then automatically moves to the end of the given string. If you do not want to stop at the first occurrence of the string, include a parameter with the F command. For example, the command 3fline locates the third occurrence of the string line (but not the first two).

CP/M text files contain both a carriage return and a line feed at the end of each line. You can refer to the combination of these two characters by including a ^L character in the search string. Give the command:

    f^LThis

to locate the string This preceded by a carriage return and a line feed—in other words, when it occurs at the beginning of a line. It is not possible to reference just a carriage return or a line feed alone.

If ED cannot find the string following the F command in the edit buffer, it displays an error message and the pointer does not move from its initial position. If this happens, check to see whether the pointer is already at the end of the buffer or if you misspelled the string.

We have seen that a very large file cannot be entirely copied into the edit buffer but must be paged through it in pieces. The F command searches only the text that is located in the edit buffer. It does not continue the search on additional text located in the original source file. Since this may sometimes be desirable, there is a second string search command that is used for large files.

The N command is similar to the F command except when the string cannot be found in the current buffer. At this point, ED automatically writes the current contents of the buffer to a disk file and then fills the buffer from the original file. ED continues searching through the entire disk file until the string has been found or until the entire original file has been searched.

At the conclusion of the N command, the pointer will be at the end of the file if the string cannot be found. In this case you should give the H command, which empties the edit buffer and restarts the editing procedure. You then issue a 0A command to copy the first part of the file into the edit buffer so you can continue.

Commands for Displaying Text in the Edit Buffer

Practically all the editing commands we have learned so far do not display the text on the console. We will now see how to view the text that is present in the edit buffer by using the T and P commands.

The T (for type) command displays lines of the edit buffer on the console video screen. If the parameter is omitted or if it is a positive number, the display begins at the character pointer. This command does not move the character pointer. Thus, if the pointer is in the middle of a line, only the right half of that line will be displayed. Figure 5.4 illustrates this command.

A negative parameter displays lines in front of the pointer. For example, the command -T shows the previous line. If the pointer is in the middle of a line, the command -T displays text from the beginning of the previous line up to the pointer. The command 0T gives the text from the beginning of the current line up to the pointer. You can obtain a printed listing of the text by engaging the printer with ^P before issuing the T command. #T will display all lines from the pointer to the end of the buffer.

The P command displays whole pages of text. However, unlike the T command, the P command moves the character pointer. If you give the P command without a parameter, one screenful of 23 lines is displayed and the pointer is placed just before the first character on the screen. (Since a videoscreen has 24 lines, this command just fills the screen.) Each time the P command is given, the next 23 lines

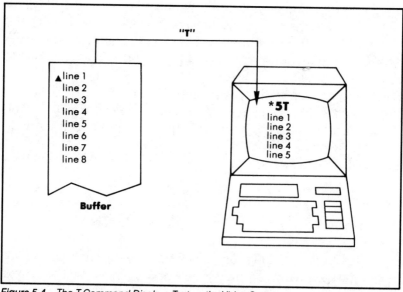

Figure 5.4 – The T Command Displays Text on the Video Screen.

are shown and the pointer is moved to the beginning of the text on the screen.

You may give a parameter to modify the P command. The command 0P displays the present page without moving the pointer. A number parameter displays that number of pages; for example, 6P displays the next six pages. A parameter of -1 displays the previous page and moves the pointer back one page. #P will display the entire buffer.

Combining Several ED Commands

Sometimes it is convenient to combine several ED commands. Most of the ED commands can be run together on the same line without spaces. However, commands that terminate the editing session must be given on a line by themselves.

We saw that when the pointer is in the middle of a line, the T command displays only the right side of the line and the 0T command displays only the left side. The combination command 0TT will display the entire line without moving the pointer. The 0T part displays text from the beginning of the line up to the pointer, and the second T displays the remainder of the line. A similar combination command, 0LT, moves the pointer to the beginning of the current line and then displays that line.

As a third example, consider the combination command B2T. This command first moves the pointer to the beginning of the buffer and then displays the first two lines of text on the video screen. Give this command and observe its effect. Notice that in addition to the two lines of text, there is a line number at the beginning of each line. Let us explore this.

Line Numbers

Each line in the edit buffer is assigned a line number that is shown on the screen but is not actually placed in the buffer. The numbers run consecutively, starting with 1. Line numbers can be used to specify where the pointer is to be moved and also to specify ranges. You can move the character pointer to a particular line by giving the line number followed by a colon. For example, the command 2: moves the pointer to line number 2.

You may specify a range of lines by giving the inclusive line numbers separated by two colons. For example, the command 2::8T displays lines 2 through 8. This form can be used only for the T and L commands we have considered and for the K command we will consider shortly.

ED normally adds line numbers when it displays text on the screen. You can disable this feature (that is, turn it off) with the -V command. The V command will turn the line numbering back on.

The command 0V is unrelated to the other two V commands. It displays two numbers. The first is the remaining free space in the edit buffer, and the second is the total buffer size. Both are given in number of bytes or characters.

The line numbers, like the character pointer, refer only to the text in the buffer. They do not appear in the edited disk file. Furthermore, when a line is deleted, the remaining lines are renumbered. Therefore, you must be careful when using line numbers from a printed listing of your file as they may not be accurate after editing. To avoid this problem, you can start editing from the bottom of the file and work upward. In this way, all the numbers from the previous version will stay the same. Let us see how this works.

Suppose you have a printout of your 100-line text containing ED's line numbers. You want to delete lines 10, 30, and 50. If you start at the top of the program, deleting line 10 first, then the line originally numbered 11 becomes 10 after the deletion. Line 12 becomes 11, line 30 becomes 29, and line 50 becomes 49. If you delete the original line 30, which is now numbered 29, all remaining line numbers will be changed again. Thus, the third line to be deleted is numbered 48 rather than the original 50.

Now suppose you reverse the process, deleting from the bottom up. If you delete line 50 first, then all lines beyond 50 are renumbered, but not those before it. The original line 30 is still 30, and the original line 10 is still 10. When line 30 is deleted next, lines numbered less than this are not changed. You can confidently delete line 10 next, since its number was not changed.

Now let us see how to alter text in the edit buffer.

COMMANDS FOR ALTERING TEXT IN THE EDIT BUFFER

In the previous sections we learned how to move the character pointer and how to display portions of the edit buffer. However, we did not actually alter the text in the buffer. In the following sections we will learn several different ways to insert and delete single characters, strings of characters, and entire lines.

Deleting Characters and Lines from the Buffer

Remember that alterations are made relative to the character pointer. The D command deletes the next character after the pointer. As with most of the commands, you may place a parameter in front of this command. For example, the command 5D deletes the five characters following the pointer, and -3D deletes the three characters in front of the pointer. The pointer is not moved by this command.

The K (for kill) command is similar to the D command except that it deletes lines rather than characters. When you give K without a parameter, text from the pointer to the end of the line is deleted. The carriage return and line feed at the end of the line are also deleted. If the pointer is in the middle of the line, K deletes only the part of the line to the right of the pointer. A command of -K deletes text from the beginning of the line up to the pointer. A positive or negative number added to K will delete more than one line. A quick way to delete all the remaining text from the pointer to the end of the buffer is to give the command #K. Be sure to use this command carefully so you don't accidentally lose more text than you intended.

Inserting Characters into the Buffer

Let us now consider ways to insert characters into the buffer. The I command is one of several commands that can be used for this purpose.

We have seen that although most of the ED commands can be given in either uppercase or lowercase letters, F and N commands must be given in lower case if the following string contains lowercase letters. In a similar way, the I command must be in lower case if you want to insert lowercase letters. If you give the I command in upper case, all the text you insert will automatically be converted to upper case.

Sometimes you will want text to be entirely upper case—for instance, if you are writing a BASIC or FORTRAN program. When you give the U command, all subsequent characters you type will be treated as upper case. (This command might be thought of as a software shift lock.) After the U command is given, you can give the I, F, and N commands in either upper or lower case, and the following characters will be treated as upper case even though they appear as lower case on the screen.

Give the -U command to reverse the effect. Then upper and lower case will be treated as distinct once again.

There are two variations of the insert command. With one method you type only the letter I and a carriage return and then enter your text on the next line. All of the following characters will be inserted into the edit buffer at the position of the character pointer. If you type another carriage return, both a carriage return and a line feed are added to the buffer. For example, the sequence:

```
i <CR>
This is the first inserted line. <CR>
This is the second line. <CR>
```

inserts two new lines in the edit buffer. The carriage return following the I command is not inserted, but the other two carriage returns are inserted, followed by line feeds. This is the normal method of creating a new file or adding large amounts of text to an existing file. Typing Escape or a ^Z terminates this form of the insert command and returns you to the command level. ED responds with the familiar asterisk. (The ^Z is not placed in the buffer.)

The second variation of the insert command is useful for adding a small number of characters to an existing file. With this method you type the letter I, follow it with the characters to be inserted, and then terminate the string of characters with an Escape or ^Z, followed by a carriage return. Neither the ^Z nor the carriage return is placed in the buffer. For example, the command:

```
iSan Francisco^Z <CR>
```

inserts the string San Francisco into the edit buffer at the position of the character pointer. The pointer then moves to the end of the string. The I command is given in lower case since the string San Francisco contains lowercase letters.

Notice that a ^Z character terminates the string. If you omit the ^Z from the end of the string, ED places both a carriage return and a line feed in the buffer and then terminates the command. In other words, the commands:

iSan Francisco <CR>

and

iSan Francisco ^L ^Z <CR>

both insert a carriage return and line feed.

Replacing One String of Characters with Another

Sometimes we need to replace one string of characters with a different string. The S (for substitute) command is used for this purpose. For example, the command:

sSan Francisco ^ZNew York ^Z

will locate the next occurrence of the string San Francisco after the character pointer and replace it with the string New York. Notice that the initial S command must be given in lower case if any of the letters in *either* string is in lower case. Also notice that one ^Z terminates the original string and a second ^Z terminates the replacement string.

You can use ^L in either string to represent the carriage return and line feed pair.

Inserting a Separate Disk File into the Buffer

We learned in Chapter 4 that you can use PIP to append one file to the end of another file. You can also perform this operation with ED using the R command. However, ED can insert one text file into any position of the text file that is being edited, not just the end. The file to be inserted may have any three-character extension, but the extension must not be blank. If you want to insert a file with the extension LIB, you may omit the extension when giving the ED command.

For example, to insert the file FILENAME.EXT during editing, move the character pointer to the desired position and give the command:

    RFILENAME.EXT <CR>

Of course, the file FILENAME.EXT continues to exist.

MOVING A BLOCK OF TEXT

Sometimes it is necessary to move a block of text from one portion of the edit buffer to another. You can do this with a combination of the X, K, and R commands. ED performs the move in several steps. The process is complicated because you must know the exact number of lines in the block. Let us look at the operation in detail, using example SAMPLE.TXT.

1. Execute ED for the file SAMPLE.TXT.

2. Move the character pointer to the beginning of the block you want to move—in this case, the beginning of the third line.

3. Determine the number of lines to be included in the block. We will move a block of three lines, so give the command:

    3T <CR>

   This displays the three lines so you can verify the block that will be moved. Remember, this command does not move the pointer or alter the text.

4. Next give the X command with the number of lines to be moved:

    3X <CR>

   The 3X command writes three lines to a temporary disk file named X$$$$$$$.LIB. The pointer does not move.

5. Give the K command to delete the corresponding block of text from the buffer. In this example the command is 3K <CR>.

6. Move the pointer to the new location. For our example, it will be following the sixth line, so the command would be 3L. Then give the command R to read the temporary file back into the edit buffer at the new position. Use the H command to end the edit and enter the changes in the disk file.

7. Finally, give the #A and #T commands to view the file. It should look like this:

   1.This is the first line of my file SAMPLE.TXT.
   2.This is the second line.
   3.This is the sixth line.
   4.This is the third line.
   5.This is the fourth line.
   6.This is the fifth line.

There is a potential problem in performing a block move. The temporary file created with the X command is automatically erased when ED is terminated. However, the temporary file is not erased when it is read with the R command. Consequently, if you give a second X command, ED will append the second block to the end of the text already present in the temporary file. Then a second R command copies both the first and the second blocks. Therefore, before performing a second block move, give the 0X command to delete the temporary file created during the first block move. Even if no temporary file exists, the 0X command will do no harm.

REPEATING GROUPS OF COMMANDS

We have seen that with some ED commands, you can give a parameter in front of a command to repeat an action. For example, 4D deletes four characters. It is also possible to give a sequence of ED commands on the same line to perform several commands at once. Sometimes it may be desirable to repeatedly execute an ED command line that contains a sequence of commands. The M (for multiple) command is used for this purpose.

For example, in the file SAMPLE.TXT give the command:

```
6sThis ^ZWhat ^Z <CR>
```

to replace the string This with the string What six times. The substitution is performed without any indication on the video screen during the operation.

We saw previously that the compound command 0TT displays a complete line. Though the command:

```
6sThis ^ZWhat ^Z0TT
```

will change This to What six times, it will display only the last line; it will not show the first five. By contrast, the command:

```
6MsThis ^ZWhat ^Z0TT
```

will display each line as the substitution is performed. With the M command ED repeatedly performs the operations indicated by the rest of the line. If you place a parameter in front of the M, ED will execute the entire line that many times. On the other hand, if there is no parameter in front of the M, ED performs the command as if the # parameter had been given; that is, the command is executed as many times as possible. Negative parameters are not valid with M. Notice that all commands following the M command up to the end of the line are included in the repeating action.

Time Delay

Sometimes the M command presents information too rapidly on the video screen. A Z (for sleep) at the end of the command will slow down the operation. A single Z pauses for about one second; an added parameter will increase the delay. For example, the command:

```
6MsThis ^ZWhat ^Z0TT2Z
```

inserts a several-second delay after each substitution. Do not confuse the Z command with ^Z.

Now let us consider several ways to end the edit session.

COMPLETING THE EDITING SESSION

Normally, you give the E command after you have finished editing a file to terminate an editing session. Several other ED commands will also end the edit.

The H command completes the editing session and saves the file, then automatically restarts the editing process. Then you can use the 0A command to add text to the buffer. You should give these commands every 10 to 15 minutes. Let us see why.

If a power failure occurs or if the computer is accidently turned off or unplugged during an editing session, the original file and the portion of the text that has been written to the new file will be intact because they are on a disk. However, you will lose the information that is contained in the edit buffer since it is in the main memory. Consequently, you should frequently force ED to transfer the information from the edit buffer to the new file by using the H command. This procedure is called *saving* a file to disk.

Sometimes a typing error causes a drastic mistake. For example, if you accidently type the command #K, all text from the pointer to the end of the buffer is deleted. In such cases you can return to a previous version of your file with the Q or O command. The Q (for quit) command returns to CP/M and abandons the changes made during the current editing session. The original file is unchanged and can be edited again, but the backup file is deleted. Be careful with this command.

The O (for original) command abandons the most recent changes. However, control remains with ED. The effect is to start the current editing session again. You must then issue the A command to fill the buffer again. When either the Q or O command is given, ED requests verification.

The Temporary ED Work File

We have seen that it is necessary to use the W command to copy lines from the edit buffer to the new file. The new file is initially given the file-name extension $$$. For example, if you are editing the file SAMPLE.TXT, ED writes the new lines to a temporary file named SAMPLE.$$$. Then at the conclusion of the editing session, ED renames the original file to SAMPLE.BAK and the new file to SAMPLE. TXT. Therefore, you should never see a file with the extension $$$. However, if your editing session is accidently interrupted, because of a power failure, for example, you will find the new version saved as SAMPLE.$$$.

When you start up CP/M as usual, give the command TYPE SAMPLE.$$$ to inspect this file. When you are convinced that it contains the edited material you want, you can change its file-name extension. (Remember, the $$$ extension marks a temporary file that might be erased at any time.) Rename the file to SAMP.TXT, a name that is slightly different from the original. You can incorporate this file into the original file by using the R command. Be sure to delete the corresponding lines of the original.

Error Messages

There are two types of error messages that might appear during an editing session. One refers to ED commands, and the other is issued by CP/M when a disk error occurs. An ED error message has the form:

BREAK X AT C

where C is the ED command being executed and X is one of the following indicators:

INDICATOR	MEANING
?C	C is an invalid command, a typographical error, or the command E, H, O, or Q combined with other commands. (Do not combine an E, H, O, or Q command with other commands.)
>	The buffer is full, or a string following an F, N, or S is too long.
#	Cannot execute F, N, or S as many times as specified.
E	Command terminated from keyboard.
0	Cannot open the LIB file for the R command. (Check to see if the LIB file exists or if you used the right file name.)
F	File error (disk or directory full).

Let us consider these messages in turn.

The ?C message is given to an invalid command—G or Y. It also appears if additional commands are placed on the same line with the E, H, O, or Q commands. (These commands must stand alone.)

The > message means that the parameter to the A command was too large, and the edit buffer was filled with text. If you only want to delete text from the buffer, there is no problem. However, it will not be possible to add new text until you write some of the buffer lines to the new disk file with the W command. Alternatively, use the H or O command to empty the buffer. Then issue the A command with a smaller parameter.

The # message means that the end of the buffer was reached before ED finished the command. This can occur, for example, if ED cannot find a string of characters specified with the F command.

The O message indicates that ED could not find the file name specified in an R command. Perhaps you misspelled the name or referenced the wrong disk.

The F message has two forms, both of which indicate a serious error. When the F is followed by the word FULL, the disk data area is full. Try to save your file to another disk using the R command. Next time, check that there is sufficient space on the disk before you begin the editing session. Alternatively, the F message will be followed by the words DIRECTORY FULL. In this case there is no more directory space, and you are likely to lose your new file.

CP/M issues the message FILE IS READ ONLY if you attempt to edit a read-only file. No harm is done. Change the file status to RW with SET and then start ED again.

You should not change the disk you are working on during the editing session. If you do, CP/M issues an error message indicating that the new disk cannot be written on. This is a serious error, as you will lose your new file.

SUMMARY

In this chapter, we have learned how to use the text editor ED. This is a general-purpose editor that allows you to modify text with just a few commands.

You will need to use ED if it is the only editor provided with your computer. Although the operation of ED is less convenient than a specialized word processor, it is a convenient tool for correcting and modifying existing files.

In learning about ED's operation, we studied the edit buffer and the commands for manipulating text in the buffer and transferring it to and from the disk. We also learned how to manipulate the character pointer, locate strings of characters, display and alter text in the edit buffer, and repeat groups of commands. A summary of the ED commands is given in Chapter 7.

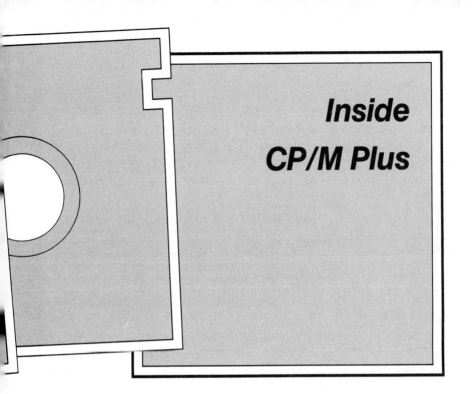

Inside
CP/M Plus

INTRODUCTION

In this chapter we present the organization of CP/M Plus in detail, including both the banked and nonbanked versions. (Since we do not discuss earlier versions of CP/M in this chapter, the shortened expression CP/M refers to CP/M Plus.) If you want to use CP/M for a specific task, such as composing a letter with an editor or solving a problem with BASIC, then you won't need the information in this chapter. On the other hand, you will want to read this chapter if you are interested in learning more about the internal operation of the system. In particular, this chapter will be useful if you want to write assembly language programs that use the resources of CP/M Plus. However, CP/M Plus is very complicated, particularly in its banked version. Alterations to CP/M itself can be very difficult and therefore are not discussed here.

Readers of this chapter are expected to be familiar with the operation of computers, including operating systems. In particular, they should understand the operation of a system editor, assembler, linking loader, and debugger. Consequently, terms such as memory buffer and base-page area will not be defined. Those who need to review this material should refer to *Mastering CP/M*.

We will first present a brief description of the logical components of CP/M, their roles, and the way they interact with each other. Then we will describe the memory allocation—that is, the way in which these software modules are arranged in memory—and the organization of the file system. Finally, we will discuss the operation of CP/M Plus in detail so that programs you write can use the resources of the system.

THE COMPONENTS OF CP/M PLUS

CP/M has three functional modules: the console command processor (CCP), the basic input-output system (BIOS), and the basic disk operating system (BDOS). Refer to Figure 6.1 as we consider each of these modules.

The Console Command Processor (CCP)

The user communicates with the CCP by entering commands at the keyboard. The CCP responds by displaying information on the video screen. The CCP also executes the user's commands by calling on the resources of the BIOS and the BDOS.

The CCP is programmed to respond to the six built-in commands DIR, DIRSYS, TYPE, RENAME, ERASE, and USER and to change the default drive. If advanced features of DIR, TYPE, RENAME, and ERASE are required, the CCP automatically loads the corresponding

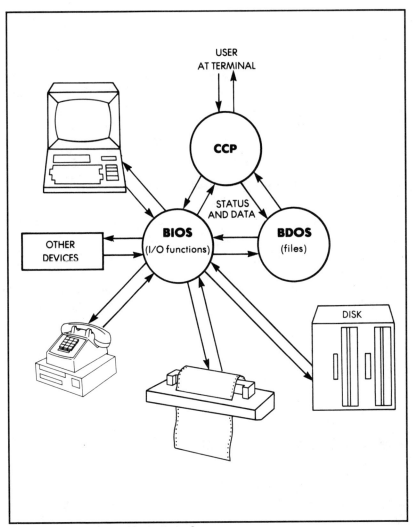

Figure 6.1 – *Interaction of CP/M with the Computer*

COM file. If a transient program is requested, the CCP loads the program and executes it.

The Basic Input-Output System (BIOS)

The *basic input-output system (BIOS)* contains the routines needed to transfer information between CP/M and the peripherals connected to the computer, including the console, the printer, the magnetic disks, and perhaps a telephone modem. The BIOS communicates primarily with the BDOS.

The BIOS must be specifically written for each different type of computer; thus, it is called device dependent. The BIOS for one computer will be different from the BIOS for another computer if the hardware is different.

The Basic Disk Operating System (BDOS)

The *basic disk operating system (BDOS)* contains the routines for operating the peripherals such as the console, printer, and disks. The BDOS also contains routines for reading and writing disk files, displaying strings of characters on the console, and generally managing the resources of the computer. The CCP and transient programs call on the BDOS to perform operations with the peripherals and to manage disk files.

The BDOS is the same for all computers running the same version of CP/M; thus it is called device independent. The BDOS calls the BIOS to perform the operations with the peripherals.

THE ORGANIZATION OF CP/M PLUS

Memory Allocation

CP/M Plus runs on 8080, 8085, and Z80 computers. These computers can only address a maximum of 64K bytes of main memory. However, it is possible to use more than 64K bytes by alternately switching one region of memory for another. This operation is called *bank switching*. The bank-switched form of CP/M Plus, which is the usual form that includes all the system's features, requires at least 128K bytes of memory and some form of memory management.

Though CP/M Plus is able to manage as many as 16 different memory banks, common implementations use only 3 banks. Furthermore, the logic needed to perform the bank switching must reside in memory that is accessible to all banks. Consequently, there is a fixed portion of memory common to all memory banks. Consider, for example, a total of 128K bytes of memory arranged as one fixed region of 32K bytes and three switchable banks of 32K bytes each. There are 64K bytes available for each combination—32K bytes are switched, and 32K bytes are common.

CP/M Plus can also be implemented with a single block of memory containing 32K–64K bytes. This *nonbanked* form is not meant to be a working version of the system but is provided to help programmers develop the banked version of CP/M. Nevertheless, it is convenient to use the nonbanked version when installing CP/M Plus on an existing computer that has only 64K bytes of memory. The disadvantage is that the nonbanked version does not incorporate all the CP/M Plus features described in this book.

Let us look at the partitioning of memory in a CP/M computer.

Partitioning of the Memory

The main memory of a CP/M Plus computer is divided into five regions: the BDOS, the BIOS, the transient program area (TPA), the memory buffer area, and the base-page area. The CCP is a separate module that resides in the TPA when it is in operation. Since the banked and nonbanked versions are arranged differently, we will describe each separately.

In the nonbanked version of CP/M Plus, a maximum of 64K bytes of memory is accessible at one time. Starting at low memory, the base-page area occupies the first 256 bytes. This region contains the entry point into the BDOS. The next region, the TPA, is the largest portion of memory. This is the area where the CCP and the transient programs are executed. The BDOS and BIOS regions are next, and the remaining memory is devoted to a buffer area for disk operations. These regions are diagrammed in Figure 6.2.

With the banked version of CP/M Plus, both the BDOS and BIOS are divided into two parts. A small portion of the BDOS and BIOS reside in the common portion of memory. The remainder is located

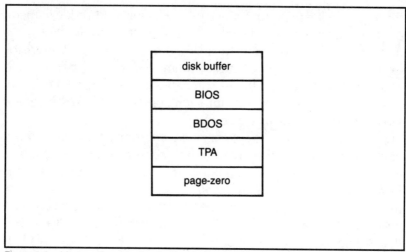

Figure 6.2 – *Memory Organization for the Nonbanked Version*

in memory bank 0. The TPA is found in both bank 1 and the common portion of memory. The page-zero region is also assigned to the beginning of bank 1. Bank 2 and any other banks are used for disk buffering. A duplicate copy of the CCP is usually kept in bank 0 or 2. Figure 6.3 shows the memory for a three-bank system.

Let us now consider the organization of the disks in CP/M Plus.

Organization of the Disks

CP/M Plus is a disk operating system. We have seen that each disk is partitioned into concentric tracks, which are further divided into sectors. A few tracks, known as the system tracks, are allocated to part of the CP/M operating system. The remainder of the disk is the data area. A small portion of the data area contains the directory listing of programs stored on the disk. The remainder of the disk is available for program storage.

The system tracks are not normally accessible. They contain the loader programs for starting CP/M each time the computer is turned on. In addition, a copy of the CCP may be located here. The remainder of CP/M—the BDOS and BIOS—are located in a regular disk file called CPM3.SYS. This portion of CP/M must be loaded into memory

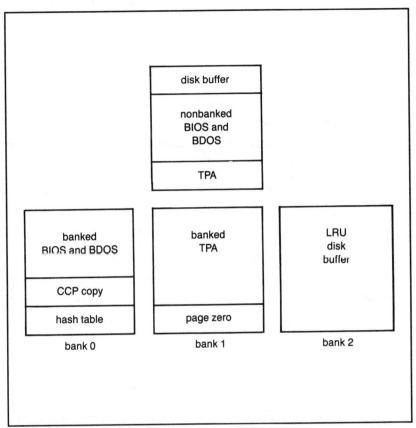

Figure 6.3 – Memory Organization for the Three-Bank Version

only when the computer is first turned on, so the CPM3.SYS file is not needed after CP/M has begun operating. If the CCP is not located on the system tracks, it is present as the file CCP.COM in the regular data area of the disk.

The files CPM3.SYS and CCP.COM may be declared as system files, so they will not appear in the regular DIR listing.

THE OPERATION OF CP/M PLUS

Now that we have learned how the memory and disk areas are organized, let us see how CP/M operates.

The File System

One of the primary functions of CP/M, as with any disk operating system (DOS), is the effective and convenient management of disk-based files. The BDOS is the part of CP/M that contains the general routines for managing the disk files.

We have seen that the disks are organized into concentric tracks. CP/M further partitions the tracks into logical sectors of 128 bytes. As we learned in Chapter 3, CP/M allocates disk space in multiples of 1K (actually 1,024) bytes, called a block or group. Depending on the disk format, a block size may be 1K, 2K, 4K, 8K, or 16K bytes. Thus, a 1K-byte block contains 8 sectors, and a 16K-byte block contains 128 sectors. Each sector is called a record. Every file on the disk consists of a collection of records.

A basic requirement of an operating system is the ability to designate a file with a symbolic name. CP/M uses a name of up to eight characters and an extension of up to three characters to designate the type of file. When a file is referenced by name, CP/M searches the disk directory until it finds a matching entry and then copies the corresponding sector into memory.

An efficient file system must include security and safety features for the period when files are being accessed. For example, files may be specified as read only or read/write. A file may require a password for access, or it may require a password to change the file but not to read it. In these cases the file is equipped with a protection device that prevents unauthorized access or execution. CP/M Plus provides all these features.

The File Control Block

Because each file may contain many records, some form of structure must be established to keep track of all the parts. For CP/M the list of blocks belonging to each disk file is contained in a special unit called a *file control block (FCB)*.

Each CP/M file is described by a 32-byte FCB, which is divided into two parts. The first part contains the file name and associated user number, file length, and attributes such as write protection. The second part of the FCB gives the locations of the blocks containing the file. Large files may need additional FCBs to specify the file location.

Each file control block is stored in the directory area of the disk. (Actually, the directory simply uses one or more of the blocks at the beginning of the data area.) Each directory sector contains four FCBs. Whenever a file is accessed, the sector containing the corresponding FCB is copied into memory. The system parameter area of main memory starting at 5C hexadecimal is the usual location for the memory version of the FCB. However, any part of the TPA may be used instead. The memory version of the FCB can be accessed quickly and conveniently by the operating system.

Each time you read or write a disk file, you must access the FCB. Therefore, let us study this device in detail.

Note that the two versions of the FCB—one located in the disk directory and the other in memory—may not always be the same. For example, when a file is created or altered, the memory FCB correctly reflects the file, but the disk FCB does not. Therefore, when it is necessary to distinguish the two versions, we will use the expressions *memory* FCB and *disk* FCB. We are now ready to identify each part, or *field*, of the FCB shown in Figure 6.4. Each byte of the 32-byte FCB is referenced by a position of 0–31.

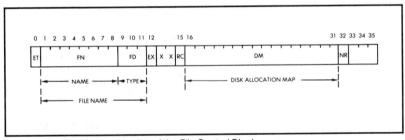

Figure 6.4 – The Memory Version of the File Control Block

FIELD	DESCRIPTION
ET (position 0):	(Disk FCB) The user number 0–F hex, or E5 hex if the file is erased. (Memory FCB) The drive identifier, where 0 = default drive, 1 = drive A, 2 = drive B.

FN (positions 1–8):   The file name, one to eight ASCII characters. If fewer than eight characters, the remainder of the field is filled with blanks.

FD (positions 9–11):   The file type, zero to three ASCII characters. If fewer than three characters, the remainder of the field is filled with blanks. Parity bits indicate attributes. The parity bit of position 9 indicates write protection. The parity bit of position 10 indicates a system file. The parity bit of position 11 indicates the archive attribute (whether a file has been altered since the last archive).

EX (position 12):   The file extent. 0 for small files. Large files require more than one FCB. This byte indicates the sequence for multiple FCBs of larger files.

XX (positions 13, 14):   These fields may be used for very large disks. Normally set to 0.

RC (position 15):   The record count. The number of 128-byte records in the extent.

DM (positions 16–31):   The disk allocation map designates the locations on disk for each block used by the file. There are 16 one-byte block numbers for small disks or 8 two-byte block numbers for large disks.

NR (position 32):   (Memory FCB only) For sequential access. The next record number to be read or written, normally 0.

When a disk file is created, the memory FCB is updated as each new block is written to the disk. However, the disk FCB is not changed at this time. Consequently, no permanent record is made until the new file is closed at the end of the write operation.

System Operation

When the computer is first turned on, the bootstrap loader built into the computer loads a larger loader, called CPMLDR, from the system tracks of drive A. The BDOS and BIOS, contained in the disk file CPM3.SYS, are copied into memory, and control is passed to the cold-start portion of BIOS. The BIOS then loads the CCP into memory. For the bank-switched version, a separate copy of the CCP is copied into bank 2 at this time. Then control is passed to the CCP so it can monitor the console keyboard for input.

If one of the six built-in commands is given at the keyboard, the CCP carries out the operation and then monitors the keyboard for another command. If a transient program is to be executed, the CCP loads the requested program into the TPA and passes control to it. This destroys the working copy of the CCP, since it resides in the TPA.

When a transient program is executed, the executing program may use the operating system resources of CP/M by performing subroutine calls to memory address 5. This address provides access to the routines of the BDOS. It is a single, fixed entry point independent of the actual memory size or types of hardware.

The call to the BDOS must be accompanied by a parameter specifying the desired operation. This parameter, called a *function number*, is contained in the C register of the 8080 or the Z80 CPU. Data are transmitted to BDOS in register E or DE, and BDOS returns information in the accumulator or the HL register.

If one or two parameters were entered with the command, the CCP constructs the beginning of file control blocks for the parameter prior to loading the program. For example, if the command line is:

    VERIFY SORT.BAS SORT.BAK

the CCP will construct one memory FCB for SORT.BAS and another for SORT.BAK. It will then copy VERIFY.COM into the TPA and execute it.

At the completion of the program, the BIOS reloads the CCP and returns control to it. If a duplicate copy of the CCP resides in bank 2, the system can rapidly restore the working version of the CCP in memory bank 1. This does not require a disk access. Alternatively, the CCP is read from the system disk in drive A. This technique takes a little longer, since a disk access is required.

Next we look at program interaction with the BDOS.

Program Interaction with BDOS

We have seen that the BDOS contains the general routines for operation of the peripherals. These routines are available to a transient program while it is operating. To use a feature of BDOS, the program places the corresponding BDOS function number in the CPU register C and the required data in register E or DE. Then the program calls the BDOS entry at address 5. The BDOS returns data in the accumulator or HL. The BDOS functions are summarized in Figure 6.5. Additional information can be found in *Mastering CP/M* (SYBEX, 1983) or the *CP/M Plus Operating System Programmer's Guide* published by Digital Research (1982).

Let us look at a few examples of BDOS calls. A transient program can send a character to the printer by placing the character in register E, the BDOS function number 5 in register C, and calling address 5. A string of characters terminated by a dollar sign can be displayed on the console screen by placing the address of the string in the DE register and function number 9 in register C. Then BDOS is called at location 5.

Accessing an Existing Disk File

Before an existing disk file can be accessed, it must be opened with BDOS function 15. The transient program places in the DE register the address of the short FCB created by CP/M. A value of 15 is placed in register C, and address 5 is called. BDOS then searches the disk directory for the corresponding file. When the file is found, CP/M fills out the remainder of the memory FCB according to the disk version

Function Number (in C)	Operation	Value Sent	Value Returned
0	Reset Disks		
1	Console input		Character in A
2	Console Output	Character in E	
3	Auxiliary input		Character in A
4	Auxiliary output	Character in E	
5	Printer output	Character in E	
6	Direct console input	FF hex	A = 0 not ready
	Direct console output	character	Character in A
7	Auxiliary input status		A = 0 not ready
8	Auxiliary output status		A = 0 not ready
9	Print console buffer	DE = address	
10	Read console buffer	DE = address	
11	Return console status		A = 0 not ready
12	Return CP/M version		Byte in A and L
13	Reset disks		
14	Select disks	E = disk	A = error code
15	Open file	DE = FCB	A = error code
16	Close file	DE = FCB	A = error code
17	Search for first	DE = FCB	A = error code
18	Search for next		A = error code
19	Delete file	DE = FCB	A = error code
20	Read sequential	DE = FCB	A = error code
21	Write sequential	DE = FCB	A = error code
22	Make new file	DE = FCB	A = error code
23	Rename file	DE = FCB	A = error code
24	Return login vector		HL = vector
25	Find default drive		A = drive
26	Set DMA address	DE = address	
27	Get alloc vector		HL = vector
28	Write protect disk		
29	Get R/O vector		HL = vector
30	Set file attributes	DE = FCB	
31	Get disk parm block		HL = block
32	Get/set user number		

Figure 6.5 – The BDOS Functions for CP/M Plus

33	Read random	DE = FCB	A = error code
34	Write random	DE = FCB	A = error code
35	Get file size	DE = FCB	A = error code
36	Set random record	DE = FCB	
37	Reset drive	DE = drive	
40	Write random/zero fill	DE = FCB	A = error code
44	Set multisector count	E = # sectors	A = error code
45	Set BDOS error mode	E = mode	
46	Get free disk space	E = drive	A = error code
47	Chain to program	E = chain flag	
48	Flush buffers	E = purge flag	A = error code
49	GET/set system control block	DE = SCB	Word in HL or byte in A
50	Direct BIOS call	DE = BIOSPB	
59	Load overlay	DE = FCB	A = error code
98	Release free blocks		
99	Truncate random file	DE = FCB	
100	Set directory label	DE = FCB	
101	Get directory label	E = drive	
102	Get date and password	DE = FCB	
103	Write file XFCB	DE = FCB	
104	Set date and time	DE = DAT address	
105	Get date and time	DE = DAT address	A = seconds
106	Set default password	DE = password addr	
107	Return serial number	DE = number field	
108	Get program return code	DE = FFFFH	HL = code
	Set program return code	DE = code	
109	Get console mode	DE = FFFFH	HL = mode
	Set console mode	DE = mode	
110	Get output delimiter	DE = FFFFH	A = value
	Set output delimiter	DE = value	
111	Print block	DE = CCB	
112	List block	DE = CCB	
152	Parse file name	DE = PFCB	

Figure 6.5 – The BDOS Functions for CP/M Plus (continues)

of the FCB. This information includes the size of the file, the attributes of the file, and the block numbers corresponding to the location of the file on the disk.

Let us consider a simple example of a BDOS call—the opening of an existing disk file. Suppose that a transient program with the file name READ.COM is designed to process a disk file given as a parameter on the command line. The command line might be:

    READ FNAME.EXT

When this command is given, CP/M constructs the first part of the FCB for the parameter FNAME.EXT at the location 5C hex. Then it loads the program READ.COM into the TPA and executes it.

Before the transient program can access the file given as the parameter, the BDOS open function must be executed. The C register is loaded with the value of 15, and the DE register is given the location of the memory FCB. A simple 8080 assembly language program to perform the open function might look like this:

```
LXI   D,5CH ;file control block
MVI   C,15 ;open function
CALL  5
INR   A
JZ    ERROR
```

The first instruction loads the DE register with the address of the memory FCB, the one set up by CP/M. The second instruction loads the C register with function number 15. The third instruction calls BDOS to perform the open function. If the requested file cannot be found in the directory, BDOS returns the value of 255 as an error message. The INR instruction changes this to zero. Thus, the zero flag will be set if there is an error. The final instruction causes a branch to an error routine in this case.

Since the BDOS does not preserve the CPU registers, a more sophisticated routine will save the registers on the stack before calling BDOS. The registers will then be restored after return from BDOS.

Creating a New Disk File

Creating a file from a memory image is a little different from reading a file. The make function, 22, is used to generate a new directory entry on the disk. Then the write function, 21, copies the file to the disk. However, at this point only the memory FCB contains the corresponding block numbers. The disk version has only the file name. Therefore, the close function, 16, must be given to update the disk FCB from the memory FCB.

Direct BIOS Calls

When you write your own computer programs, you can indirectly access the console, the printer, and the disks through the BDOS entry point at address 5. With previous versions of CP/M, it was also possible to access these peripherals directly through the BIOS entry point at address 0. However, with the banked version of CP/M Plus, the BIOS is not located in the same bank as the TPA. Consequently, executing programs cannot use this technique. If it is necessary to directly access the BIOS, you can use BDOS function 50 to perform the operation.

SUMMARY

The organization and operations of CP/M have been described in this chapter.

We learned that CP/M has three major parts—the CCP, the BDOS, and the BIOS—and we learned how the parts interact with each other. We also learned how the CCP interacts with the user. In addition, we saw how executing programs can use the peripherals and the disk file system by calling on the BDOS. In particular, we studied the form of the file control block that keeps track of each disk file.

A Quick
Reference to
CP/M Commands
and Programs

INTRODUCTION

This chapter provides a quick reference guide to all CP/M Plus commands and programs, even those that are not described elsewhere in this book. The commands are arranged in alphabetical order, with each beginning on a new page. The keyword at the top of the page will help you locate the commands quickly. In addition, information is organized into consistent categories within each section for easy reference.

Each command is introduced by a brief statement describing its purpose. It is then identified as built-in, transient, or a combination of the two. Next, the format of the command is presented through examples.

Note that when a file-name parameter is shown in the form PNAME, you must give only the primary part of the file name; you do not include the extension. When a parameter is given in the form PNAME.EXT, then you must enter both the primary name and the extension. When a parameter refers to a file on the default drive, you need not append the drive name to the file name. However, when the file is not on the default drive, you must include the drive name with the file name.

The symbol D: by itself means that you are to enter only the disk name followed by a colon. The expression *ambig* indicates that you can include the ? and * ambiguous symbols in the file name to reference more than one file. The expression [option] means that you may give one or more options, enclosed in a single pair of square brackets. Alternatively, a particular option may be shown as [FULL]. The left bracket immediately follows the previous parameter or command with no intermediate space.

Following the format is a description of the command. Some commands also include brief comments on how to use the command or text reference for further information.

Remember that this chapter is for quick reference use. If you need more detailed explanation of a command, turn to the chapter in the text where it is discussed.

COPY	*Duplicate an entire disk*
	(COPY.COM transient)

FORMAT:

COPY

DESCRIPTION:

This program duplicates entire disks by performing three operations—formatting a new disk, copying the system tracks, and copying the files. This is the fastest method for making duplicate copies of complete disks. However, COPY is not a standard CP/M program, so it may not be available on your computer. In that case you use the three separate programs FORMAT, COPYSYS, and PIP to duplicate a disk. COPY must be specifically written for your computer; do not use a version from a different computer.

Sometimes COPY also incorporates a separate formatting program (see FORMAT).

USE:

The operation will vary from one computer to another. Execute COPY and follow its instructions. Remove the system disk from drive A and replace it with the disk you want to copy. Place the new disk in drive B. At end of the copy operation, remove both disks. Make copies of other original disks by repeating the operation; you do not have to restart COPY for each duplication.

Be careful not to copy backward—that is, from the new disk in drive B to the original in drive A. You can destroy the information on an original disk by copying backward from the new disk to the original disk.

Replace a copy of your system disk into drive A before terminating the COPY program.

See Chapter 2 for more details.

COPYSYS	*Copy the system tracks from one disk to another. Also copy the system file CPM3.SYS.*
	(COPYSYS.COM transient)

FORMAT:

COPYSYS

DESCRIPTION:

For CP/M Plus to run, both the part of CP/M on the system tracks and the system file CPM3.SYS must be on the system disk that is in drive A. They need not be on other disks used only in other drives. The COPYSYS program copies the system tracks from one disk to another. It can also copy the system file CPM3.SYS. COPYSYS must be written specifically for your computer; do not use a version from a different computer.

USE:

Execute the COPYSYS program and follow the directions. The program will ask where to get a copy of the system with a statement such as:

Source drive name (or return for default):

Respond with the name of the drive containing the CP/M system (normally drive A). If the source disk is on the default drive, just enter a carriage return. You are then asked to insert the source disk into the selected drive and press <CR>.

COPYSYS next asks for the destination drive, the disk where a copy of the system is to be written. The expression might be:

Destination drive name (or return for default):

Respond with the name of the destination drive, the disk where the system is to be written (normally drive B). If this is the default drive, just give a carriage return. You are asked to insert the destination disk into the selected drive and type return.

For the third phase COPYSYS asks:

Do you wish to copy CPM3.SYS?

Answer Y to this request, and COPYSYS copies this file to the destination drive. COPYSYS then cycles so you can place the CP/M system on additional disks.

See Chapter 2 for further details.

DATE	*Display and set date and time*
	(DATE.COM transient program)

FORMAT:

    DATE
    DATE CONTINUOUS
    DATE SET
    DATE MM/DD/YY HH:MM:SS

DESCRIPTION:

This program displays and alters the date and time.

USE:

When you execute the command without a parameter, CP/M presents a single display of the day of the week; the month, day, and year; and the time in hours, minutes, and seconds. For example:

    Mon 07/04/83 11:15:33

In the previous example the date and time are displayed, then control returns to CP/M. However, if you want to watch the displayed time change in accordance with the actual time, give the parameter CONTINUOUS or its abbreviation, C. Then the display will emulate a digital clock. No other task can be performed while this is happening. Press any key to terminate the program.

The date and time can be altered in one of two ways. If you give the parameter SET, the program asks for the date and the time separately. You can skip over one if want to change only the other. Alternatively, you can specify the complete date and time in the parameter with a command such as:

    DATE 07/04/83 11:15:83

Choose a time that is a few minutes ahead. The time and date will be set and then the message:

Press any key to set time

will appear. Press the space bar at the correct time. Notice that you do not enter the day of the week when setting the date. The program calculates this for you. Since the clock is not usually battery powered, you must reset the date and time each time the computer is turned on or reset. This task can be simplified by adding the line:

DATE SET

to the end of the PROFILE.SUB file. Then CP/M will automatically ask you for the date and time each time you perform a cold boot.

DEVICE	*Display and alter peripheral assignments*
	(DEVICE.COM transient program)

FORMAT:

```
DEVICE NAMES
DEVICE VALUES
DEVICE CONOUT: = CRT,PRNTR
DEVICE CON:[PAGE]
DEVICE CON:[COLUMNS = nn, LINES = mm]
DEVICE LST: = PRNTR[NOXON,2400]
DEVICE
```

DESCRIPTION:

This program is used to display and alter the mapping of the logical devices CON:, LST:, and AUX: to the actual peripheral devices such as console, printer, and modem. It is possible to map one logical device to more than one peripheral. For example, console output can be sent simultaneously to both the console and the printer. DEVICE can change the number columns and lines that are displayed on the console.

USE:

The use of this command is dependent on the number of peripherals attached to your computer and the device names selected by the manufacturer.

When DEVICE is executed with the NAMES parameter, a listing of the peripheral devices and their transfer rate is given. These names are assigned by the computer manufacturer and so will be different from one computer to the next. DEVICE executed with the VALUES parameter shows the current mapping of these devices to the CP/M logical devices. The result might be:

```
CONIN: = CRT
CONOUT: = CRT
AUXIN: = MODEM
AUXOUT: = MODEM
LST: = PRNTR
```

The devices CONIN: and CONOUT: refer respectively to conole input and output. The abbreviated form CON: refers to both. CONSOLE and KEYBOARD are synonymous with CON:. (Notice that there is no colon at the end of these two names.) Similarly, PRINTER is synonymous with LST:. DEVICE executed with the CONOUT parameter makes output appear at both the printer and the console. Refer to the PUT and GET commands for similar operations.

The [PAGE] option shows the current number of columns and lines displayed on the video screen. The next option sets the video display size to the number of columns and lines you wish.

The transfer rate can be changed by the mapping command. For example, the command:

```
DEVICE LST: = PRNTR[NOXON, 2400]
```

maps the PRNTR to the logical printer and sets the transfer rate to 2,400. You must also select either XON to enable the X-ON protocol or NOXON to disable it. Generally, you want NOXON unless an X appears in the NAMES listing.

DEVICE executed without a parameter lists both the output from the NAMES parameter and the output from the VALUES parameter. Then the program waits for your input.

For further explanation, see Chapter 3.

DIR	*Display a list of file names in the disk directory. Determine file size and file attributes*
	(Built-in command and DIR.COM extension)

FORMAT:

Built-in

    DIR
    DIR D:
    DIR PNAME.EXT
    DIR *ambig*

Transient Extension

    DIR[option]
    DIR PNAME.EXT[option]
    DIR *ambig*[option]

DESCRIPTION:

DIR is a very versatile program that is used to list the disk files and their characteristics. The built-in version can be executed from any drive and user area, but its features are limited, producing a simple listing of all nonsystem file names that match the file-name parameter. There are four forms of this version. The ambiguous ? and * symbols may be included in the name. If no parameter is given, all nonsystem files belonging to the current user are listed.

Options given in brackets increase the power of DIR. When options are included, the names are sorted in alphabetical order. Other specific functions of individual options are summarized in the complete listing of DIR options below.

If no files match the specification, the message NO FILE appears. If system files are present, the message SYSTEM FILE(S) EXIST is shown.

OPTIONS:

Be sure to place options within square brackets when giving the command.

OPTION	FUNCTION
ATT	Display user-defined file attributes.
DATE	List files with date and time (if activated).
DIR	List only nonsystem files (default).
DRIVE=ALL	List files for all logged-in drives.
DRIVE=A	List files for specified drive.
DRIVE=(A,B)	List files for specified drives.
EXCLUDE	List files that do not match file name.
FF	Insert form-feed character at start of listing.
FULL	List files with complete description.
LENGTH=n	Place heading after n lines.
MESSAGE	Display names of disks and user areas as they are processed.
NOPAGE	Display listing continuously.
NOSORT	Do not sort listing alphabetically.
RO	List only files that are read only.
RW	List only files that are read/write.
SIZE	Show size of each file.
SYS	List only system files.
USER=ALL	List files for all user areas.
USER=2	List files for specified user.
USER=(2,3)	List files for specified users.

USE:

See Chapter 3 for a detailed explanation of how to use DIR.

DIRSYS	*Directory listing of system files*
	(Built-in command)

FORMAT:

    DIRSYS
    DIRSYS D:
    DIRSYS PNAME.EXT
    DIRSYS *ambig*

DESCRIPTION:

This built-in program is a variation of DIR that provides a simple listing of system files. The DIR command with option parameters can also list system files. However, DIRSYS is faster since it is a built-in command. This command may be abbreviated DIRS.

USE:

See Chapter 3 for a description of how to use DIRSYS.

DUMP	Display nontext files in both hexadecimal and ASCII
	(DUMP.COM transient program)

FORMAT:

DUMP
DUMP PNAME.EXT

DESCRIPTION:

Text files can be examined with the TYPE command or with a system editor such as ED. However, nontext files such as COM, REL, and OVR files must be processed before they can be studied. DUMP produces a listing in both hexadecimal and ASCII that can be displayed on the console or the printer.

The DUMP program is useful for assembly language programmers.

ED	*Edit a text file*
	(ED.COM transient program)

FORMAT:

    ED
    ED PNAME.EXT
    ED PNAME.EXT D:

DESCRIPTION:

The ED program is a simple line-oriented text editor. It can create and alter text files used for computer programs, letters, and reports. It does not include a video screen mode, nor does it provide word processing features such as justification, subscripting, and boldfacing.

USE:

The operation of ED is described in detail in Chapter 5. A brief summary of the commands is given here. For explanation of how to use the commands in combination, see Chapter 5.

In the following list, n specifies the number of times a command is to be repeated. If n is omitted, a value of 1 is usually assumed. The # symbol is used to indicate a large, unspecified number. The +/- symbol means that n may be either a positive or a negative number. The plus sign is normally omitted from a positive number.

COMMAND	EXPLANATION
nA	Copy (append) n lines from the source file to the end of the text in the edit buffer.
0A	Copy lines from the source file until edit buffer is half filled.
B	Move pointer to beginning of buffer.
-B	Move pointer to end of buffer.

+/-nC	Move pointer forward (+) or backward (-) n characters.
+/-nD	Delete n characters forward (+) or backward (-) from the pointer.
E	End the edit session normally.
Fstring^Z	Find the next occurrence of the given string in the edit buffer, starting at the original pointer position. If the string is found, move the pointer to the end of the string. Otherwise, the pointer is not moved. The F command must be given in lower case if lowercase letters are included in the string. Only the edit buffer is searched. See the N command.
nFstring^Z	Find the nth occurrence of the given string.
H	Save all changes in a temporary disk file and then restart the edit.
I	Insert text in front of the pointer. You normally give the command in lower case because if I is given in upper case, all inserted text is converted to upper case. Press escape or ^Z to terminate the command.
IText^Z	Insert a short string of characters. I must be in lower case if inserted text has lowercase letters.
nJfstring^Zistring^Zdstring^Z	Find fstring, delete text up to but not including dstring, then insert istring. (J indicates juxtapose.)
+/-nK	Delete (kill) n lines starting (+) or ending (-) at the pointer.

+ /-nL	Move pointer to the beginning of the current line and then move it n lines forward (+) or backward (-).
0L	Move pointer to beginning of current line.
nMcommandstring	Repeat (multiple) execution of the command string n times. If n is omitted or has a value of 0 or 1, execute the command string repeatedly until an error occurs. See also the Z command.
Nstring ^Z	Find the next occurrence of the given string starting at the original position of the pointer. If the string is found, move the pointer to the end of the string. In contrast to the F command, if the string is not found in the buffer, ED searches the original file on disk. The N command must be given in lower case if lowercase letters are included in the string. See the F command.
nNstring ^Z	Find the nth occurrence of the given string.
O	Abort (omit) the editing session and return to original source file. The new changes are discarded, and the edit buffer is emptied.
+ /-nP	Move pointer n pages and display the page following the pointer.
0P	Display page following the pointer. The pointer is not moved.
Q	Abort editing session, discarding all changes. The original file is intact, but the backup is deleted.
RPNAME.EXT	Read the given disk file into the buffer at the pointer position. If the file type is LIB, it may be omitted from the

command. A file with no file type cannot be read. If the entire file name is omitted, X$$$$$$$.LIB is assumed.

nSoldtext ^Znewtext ^Z   Starting at pointer position, substitute newtext for the next occurrence of oldtext. Repeat n times. The S command must be given in lower case if any of the letters in either string is in lower case.

+ /-nT   Display (type) n lines of text on screen, starting (+) or ending (-) at pointer. The pointer is not moved.

0T   Display text from beginning of line to pointer. Pointer is not moved.

U   Translate lowercase input to uppercase until the -U command is given.

-U   Turn off uppercase translation. Upper and lower case are preserved.

V   Add line numbers to display but not to text in buffer.

-V   Turn off display of line numbers.

0V   Display the number of remaining bytes in the buffer and the total size of the buffer.

nW   Copy (write) n lines from the buffer to the new file and delete the corresponding lines from the buffer. Not needed when the session is ended with the E command.

nXPNAME.EXT   Copy the next n lines of text to the end of the file named PNAME.EXT if it exists. Otherwise, create a new file. The corresponding lines remain intact in the buffer. If the extension is omitted, LIB is assumed. If the entire file

	name is omitted, X$$$$$$$.LIB is assumed.
0XPNAME.EXT	Delete the file PNAME.EXT. If the file name is omitted, X$$$$$$$.LIB is assumed.
nZ	Suspend operation for approximately one second. An n parameter indicates a specific number of seconds. Used with the M command.
+/-n	Move the pointer ahead or back n lines and display that line.
n:	Move pointer to beginning of line number n.
n1::n2	Specify a range of line numbers beginning with n1 and ending with n2. If either n1 or n2 is omitted, the current line number is assumed. Use only with K, L, and T commands.

ERASE	Erase disk files
	(Built-in command and ERASE.COM extension)

FORMAT:

Built-in

ERASE
ERASE PNAME.EXT
ERASE *ambig*

Transient Extension

ERASE PNAME.EXT[CONFIRM]
ERASE *ambig*[CONFIRM]

DESCRIPTION:

This command erases files that match the file name. Of course, write-protected files and files on a disk that is designated as read only cannot be erased. Only files in the current user area can be erased. When the ambiguous symbols ? and * are included, ERASE repeats the file name and requests permission to proceed. When the option parameter is given, ERASE requests permission to erase each separate file. If ERASE cannot find a file to match the given parameter, it displays the message NO FILE.

USE:

ERASE executed without the option parameter is a built-in command, so it can be run from any disk drive and any user area. When the option parameter is included, the transient extension is required. ERASE.COM must exist on the current drive, a drive name must be included, or a search path must be previously established with SETDEF.

This command may be abbreviated to ERA, and the confirm option can be abbreviated to C. Below are some examples of the ERASE command. For further information, see Chapter 3.

ERASE SAMPLE.TXT	(erase file on current disk)
ERASE B:SAMPLE.TXT	(erase file on drive B)
ERA *.BAK[CONFIRM]	(erase all backup files with confirmation)

FORMAT	Format a new disk
	(FORMAT.COM transient)

FORMAT:

FORMAT

DESCRIPTION:

A new disk must be formatted before it is used for the first time. It also may be necessary to reformat a disk if the power fails during a write operation. FORMAT is not a standard CP/M program, so it may not be available on your system. FORMAT must be specifically programmed for your computer; do not use a version from a different computer. If you cannot find FORMAT.COM, execute COPY.COM and see if it has a formatting capability.

This program destroys any information on the disk surface. Be careful not to accidently format a working disk.

USE:

FORMAT cycles, so you can format several new disks one after the other.

For more details, see Chapter 2.

GENCOM	Create a special version of CP/M Plus
	(GENCOM.COM transient program)

FORMAT:

   GENCOM

DESCRIPTION:

This program is used by programmers to create a custom version of CP/M Plus or to add new CP/M features.

GET	Get console input from a disk file
	(GET.COM transient program)

FORMAT:

GET CONSOLE INPUT FROM FILE PFILE.EXT
GET CONSOLE INPUT FROM CONSOLE
GET CONSOLE INPUT FROM FILE PFILE.EXT[SYSTEM]
GET FILE PFILE.EXT[NOECHO]

DESCRIPTION:

With the GET command it is possible to input information from a disk file rather than from the console.

USE:

The first form of the GET command instructs CP/M to execute the next command or program given at the console. Then if console input is needed, it is to be taken from the disk file named PFILE.EXT rather than from the console. Input is again taken from the console when the program terminates or when all the commands in the disk file have been executed.

The second form of the GET command, either placed into the file PFILE.EXT or given from the console, returns console input to its normal mode. The third form of the command immediately switches console input to the given disk file so that the command line can also be read from the disk file.

As commands are read from the disk file, they are normally displayed (echoed) on the video screen as though they were typed from the keyboard. This display can be suppressed with the option NO ECHO, shown in the fourth form of the command. The words CONSOLE INPUT FROM may be omitted from any form of the GET command. Refer to SUBMIT for a similar operation.

HELP	Learn more about CP/M commands and programs
	(HELP.COM and HELP.HLP transients)

FORMAT:

HELP
HELP topic
HELP topic subtopic
HELP topic[option]
HELP.subtopic
HELP[option]

DESCRIPTION:

You can execute the transient program HELP.COM, with its gigantic work file, HELP.HLP, to learn more about CP/M Plus commands and programs. Since it is not possible to use the HELP program while another program is executing, it may be more useful to refer to this book when you have a problem.

USE:

When executed without a parameter, HELP produces a list of topics that are available. You can then enter the desired subtopic in response to the HELP prompt. If you choose a subtopic directly, insert a period at the beginning of the response.

The listing stops after the screen fills. To continue the listing, press the carriage return. Alternatively, you can obtain a printed listing by toggling the printer with ^P. In this case, give either the NOPAGE or the LIST option so that the listing will continue automatically. The NOPAGE option leaves gaps at the end of each page, whereas the LIST option prints continuously.

The HELP.HLP work file contains the text that is displayed on the console. However, the text is not in a form that can be altered with a system editor like ED, since some of the characters are not ASCII. Therefore, you must use the EXTRACT option to create a HELP.DAT work file that can be edited. Alternatively, you can create your own HELP.DAT file containing new material. Then use the CREATE option to combine your HELP.DAT file with the original HELP.HLP file.

HEXCOM	*Generate an executable COM file from an Intel HEX file*
	(HEXCOM.COM transient program)

FORMAT:

HEXCOM PNAME
HEXCOM

DESCRIPTION:

This is a routine for assembly language programmers. MAC produces files in the Intel hexadecimal format. HEXCOM creates a transient COM file from the corresponding HEX file. See the MAC command.

INITDIR	Prepare disk directory for date and time labeling
	(INITDIR.COM transient program)

FORMAT:

INITDIR D:

DESCRIPTION:

CP/M Plus can encode two different values of time and date for each file in the disk directory. (This is sometimes called date and time tagging, or stamping.) The information is stored not with the regular directory entry, but in a separate section of the directory. Furthermore, the directory area must be specially prepared for time and date tagging. Consequently, the INITDIR command should be given immediately after a new disk is formatted and before any files have been saved. There must be sufficient directory space for the new time and date listings.

Run the program SET to choose the mode of date and time tagging or to disable this feature.

USE:

Execute INITDIR with the desired disk parameter. Since INITDIR alters the directory, the program asks for confirmation of the command. Furthermore, if the power should go off while you are reformatting the directory, you can lose your files, so be sure to make a backup disk before executing INITDIR.

LIB	Create and edit a library of compiled subroutines
	(LIB.COM transient program)

FORMAT:

    LIB PNAME.EXT[options]

DESCRIPTION:

Many Pascal, FORTRAN, COBOL, and BASIC compilers and the RMAC and MACRO-80™ assemblers produce relocatable modules with the file extension REL or IRL. A collection of useful routines can be combined into a single library using the program LIB. Refer to instructions for these languages.

LINK	Create an executable file from relocatable modules
	(LINK.COM transient program)

FORMAT:

LINK PNAME, PNAME2, PNAME, . . .[options]

DESCRIPTION:

Many PASCAL, FORTRAN, COBOL, and BASIC compilers and the RMAC and MACRO 80 assemblers produce relocatable modules with the file extension REL. A collection of modules can be combined into an executable COM file with LINK. Refer to instructions for these languages.

MAC™	Macroassembler for assembly language programs
	(MAC.COM transient)

FORMAT:

    MAC PNAME
    MAC PNAME $options

DESCRIPTION:

The macroassembler MAC creates three new files from an assembly language source program and an optional macro library. The source program has a file type ASM, and the macro library has the type LIB. The assembled code is written to a HEX file, the symbol table is found in a SYM file, and the printer listing is a PRN file. The separate program HEXCOM creates an executable file from the HEX file (see HEXCOM).

A dollar sign symbol rather than the usual square bracket precedes the command line options. A space must precede the dollar sign. If no options are given, all files are referenced to the default drive. However, any other drive can be selected using the appropriate options. See a macro assembler manual and *Mastering CP/M* (SYBEX, 1983) for more details. Also see RMAC.

PATCH	Install revision to CP/M Plus or a program
	(PATCH.COM transient program)

FORMAT:

    PATCH PNAME
    PATCH PNAME n

DESCRIPTION:

When a major revision to a computer program is necessary, the program may be completely replaced with a separate version. However, minor revisions to the CP/M Plus operating system or to existing transient programs can be performed by overlaying the changes to a memory version of the original. Then the revised version is saved to disk. This process is known as *patching,* and the file containing the changes is called a *patch.*

Patches can be automatically installed by executing PATCH with the corresponding patch routine supplied by Digital Research. If more than one revision has been issued, they are referenced by patch numbers starting with 1.

PATCH can either install a patch or indicate whether a patch has been installed.

PIP	Copy disk files and transfer files between peripherals
	(PIP.COM transient)

FORMATS:

```
PIP
PIP PNAME2.EXT = PNAME1.EXT[option]
PIP ambig1 = ambig2[option]
PIP D: = PNAME.EXT[option]
PIP LARGE = SMAL1,SMAL2,SMAL3
```

DESCRIPTION:

PIP, which stands for peripheral interchange program, can copy a disk file, concatenate several files into a new file, send a disk file to the console or printer, or transfer a file from one peripheral to another. A file can be altered during the copy operation by making all letters lower or upper case, zeroing the parity bit, adding line numbers, and expanding the tab character. A portion of a file can be extracted and made into a smaller separate file. The file can be displayed on the console during transfer.

Chapter 4 is entirely devoted to the operation of PIP. A summary of how to use the command is included here, and the option parameters are listed. Refer to Chapter 4 if you need more detailed explanation of any PIP operation or option.

USE:

PIP can be executed with or without parameters. In the latter case PIP presents an asterisk prompt so that you can give a sequence of commands. Each PIP command contains two file-name parameters separated by an equals sign. PIP creates the destination file (the first parameter) from the source file (the second parameter). There may also be option parameters surrounded by a single pair of square brackets. In this case the left square bracket must immediately follow the file-name parameter without a space.

The following example commands show how PIP works in various cases. Assume A is the default drive.

To copy a single file from one disk to another, give the command:

    PIP B: = PNAME.EXT[V] <CR>

The V option parameter forces PIP to verify that the copy is correct.

To copy a collection of files from drive A to drive B, give the command:

    PIP B: = PNAME?.*[V] <CR>

where the ambiguous ? and * symbols can match several files.

To copy all files from A to B, give the command:

    PIP B: = *.*[V] <CR>

To duplicate a file with a different name on the default disk, give the command:

    PIP PNAME2.NEW = PNAME1.OLD[V] <CR>

To concatenate two files into a new single file, give the command:

    PIP PNAME3.NEW = PNAME1.OLD[V],PNAME2.OLD[V] <CR>

To copy a file from the default drive and default user area to drive B and user area 2, give the command:

    PIP B:[G2] = PNAME.EXT[V] <CR>

To extract a portion of a text file, give the commands:

    PIP <CR>
    PSHORT.EXT = PFULL.EXT[Sstart ^Z Qstop ^Z] <CR>

The new file PSHORT.EXT will contain the text from the string start through the string stop. If lowercase letters appear in either string, PIP must be executed initially without a parameter. Notice that each string is terminated by a ^Z.

OPTION PARAMETERS:

The following list summarizes the PIP option parameters. See Chapter 4 for more detailed explanation.

PIP options are enclosed in a single pair of square brackets. The left bracket immediately follows the file-name parameters without a space. The options may be placed in any order and separated by spaces or run together. Note that in the list the letter n stands for an unspecified number. For example, n columns means the number of columns you will enter with the parameter.

A   Archive mode. Copies only files that have been modified since the previous archive copy operation. The file name of the copied file is altered so the file will not be copied next time.

C   Confirm. Request permission to copy each file that matches an ambiguous file name.

Dn   Delete after n columns. PIP deletes characters that extend beyond n characters of each line. Use this parameter to reduce the length of long lines if you are sending a file to a narrow printer or video screen. Very long lines are not handled correctly. The tab character must be expanded with the T option. Use only for text files.

E   Display (echo) text on console. Normally, disk-to-disk transfers are invisible. If you want to investigate the operation of several of the PIP parameters described in this section, especially those that alter the file, it may be helpful to observe the copying operations on the video screen as it is being performed. Do not use with the N option. Use only for text files.

F   Filter (remove) form feeds. The ASCII form-feed character, ^L, appears in certain types of files to indicate when to start a new page. Some printers will properly begin a new page when this character is encountered. However, for other types of printers you should use the F option to remove the form-feed character. Also use the F parameter with the P parameter to change the page size. Use only for text files.

Gn   Move (get) a file to or from user area n. PIP copies the file from the specified user area to the current user area. Place the option after the destination file name, the first parameter, to copy a file from the current user area to user area n. This is the only option that can appear after the first parameter. The value of n can range from 0 to 15. For example, the command:

    PIP B:[G2] = A:SORT.BAS[G3]

copies the file from user area 3 on disk A to user area 2 on disk B.

H   Hexadecimal data transfer. Always give this parameter whcn transferring HEX filos. PIP then checks all data for proper Intel® hexadecimal format. Use only for HEX files. For more information see my book *Mastering CP/M* (SYBEX, 1983).

I   Ignore HEX end-of-file record. When concatenating HEX files, include this parameter for each file but the last. This option automatically sets the H option. Use the H option on the last file. For example, the command:

    PIP NEW.HEX = FIRST.HEX[I],SECOND.HEX[I],
    THIRD[H]

concatenates three HEX files. Use only for HEX files.

K   Omit (kill) display of file names during transfer. When the file-name parameter is ambiguous, PIP displays the word COPYING and then lists each file as it is transferred. The K option disables this feature.

L   Translate to lower case. All uppercase letters are changed to the corresponding lower case. Other characters are unchanged. Give the command:

    PIP CON: = FILE.TEX[L] <CR>

to observe the action on the console. Use only for

text files. The Z option must be included for WordStar files.

N	Add line numbers. Numbers are inserted at the beginning of each line of a new file. The numbers begin with 1 and are incremented by one. Blanks fill out the field to six characters, and a colon and blank are placed after each number. This parameter is useful for referencing the lines of a listing. Do not use both the N and E options. WordStar text files are incorrectly numbered unless the Z option is also given. Use only for text files.

N2	Add BASIC line numbers. Lines of the file are numbered as with the N parameter. However, zeros are used to fill the line instead of blanks, and an ASCII tab character follows each number instead of a colon and blank. (The tab character can be expanded to the corresponding number of spaces by using the T option.) Use only for text files.

O	Object (nontext) file transfer. You must use this parameter when you concatenate nontext, non-COM files, but it is not needed for copying any file or for concatenating COM files. Do not use for text files.

Pn	Set page length. PIP inserts the ^L form-feed character at the beginning of the new file and after every n lines. If n is omitted or has a value of 1, form feeds are inserted every 60 lines. (This is the default specification.) The F parameter should also be given so that any existing form feeds are removed. The printer you are using must respond to the form-feed character, or this parameter will have no effect. Use only for text files.

Qstring ^Z	Quit at this string. This parameter directs PIP to copy a file up to and including the given string. The string can be any regular keyboard character(s). A ^Z character marks the end of the string. Execute the command on two lines as shown below to keep

lowercase letters. A one-line command will convert lowercase letters to upper case. For example, the commands:

PIP
CON: = FILE.TXT[QWashington. ^Z]

will display FILE.TXT on the video screen up to and including the expression Washington. Use only for text files. See the S option for starting strings.

R Copy (read) system files. Files marked as system files are not displayed with the DIR command and are not normally copied by PIP. Therefore, when making a backup copy of the system disk, you should give the R parameter. For example, the command:

PIP B: = A: *.*[VR]

copies all files including system files from drive A to drive B.

Sstring^Z Start at this string. This parameter directs PIP to start copying when it encounters the given string. The string can include any regular keyboard character(s). A ^Z character marks the end of the string. Execute the command on two lines as shown below to keep lowercase letters. A one-line command will convert lowercase letters to upper case. For example, the commands:

PIP
CON: = FILE.TXT[SToday ^Z]

will display FILE.TXT on the video screen starting with the expression Today. Use only for text files. See the Q option for quitting strings.

Tn Expand tabs. CP/M automatically expands the ASCII tab character, ^I, to eight-column fields by the addition of spaces when a file is displayed on the video screen. However, when a file is printed with the PIP device LST:, the tab character is copied unchanged. The T parameter can be included in a PIP command to expand the tab character to every nth column. PIP does this by adding spaces. Tabs are commonly used in assembly language and Pascal programs. For example, the command:

PIP LST: = BIOS.ASM[T8]

will print the file BIOS.ASM and expand tabs to eight-column fields. Use only for text files.

U   Translate to upper case. All lowercase letters are changed to the corresponding upper case. Other characters are unchanged. Give the command:

PIP CON: = FILE.TEX[U] <CR>

to observe the action on the console. Use only for text files. The Z option must be included for files prepared with WordStar.

V   Verify. This option directs PIP to verify that a new file has been correctly written. It should be used for all disk-to-disk transfers but not for transfers to peripheral devices such as CON: or LST:. An error message is displayed if the copy is incorrect.

W   Write over (delete) read-only files. Disk files can be write protected against accidental deletion by setting the RO attribute. Normally, when PIP creates a new file, it checks to see if a file with the same name already exists. If there is such a file and it is not write protected, PIP will automatically erase it. If the existing file is write protected, PIP will print the error message:

DESTINATION IS R/O, DELETE (Y/N)?

and wait for your response. You answer Y to continue or N to quit. However, if you include the W option, PIP will automatically delete write-protected files on the destination drive without asking for permission.

Z   Zero the parity bit. The ASCII character set only uses seven bits. Consequently, the remaining bit of each byte, called the *parity bit,* can be used as an error check. However, sometimes this bit is used for other purposes. For example, WordStar in the document mode sets the parity bit to indicate spacing for justification. On the other hand, Microsoft BASIC requires the parity bit to be reset. Thus, if a BASIC program is edited with the document mode of WordStar, the parity bit will be set for many of the characters and the BASIC program can no longer be used. When this happens, use the Z option of PIP to restore the BASIC program to its original form by zeroing the parity bit. For example, the command:

    PIP SORT.BAS = SORT.BAS[VZ]

will make the program SORT.BAS usable again. Notice that in this example both the original file and the new file have the same name. Do not use ambiguous characters in this case or you may lose your file. The Z parameter is not needed for transfer to ASCII devices such as CON: and LST: and it must *not* be used for copying binary files or WordStar files.

PUT	*Put console output or printer output into a disk file*
	(PUT.COM transient program)

FORMAT:

>   PUT CONSOLE OUTPUT TO FILE PFILE.EXT[option]
>   PUT PRINTER OUTPUT TO FILE PFILE.EXT[option]
>   PUT CONSOLE OUTPUT TO CONSOLE
>   PUT PRINTER OUTPUT TO PRINTER

DESCRIPTION:

CP/M normally sends console output to the console and printer output to the printer. The PUT command can send console and printer output to a disk file as well.

USE:

The first and second forms of the PUT command instruct CP/M to create a disk file named PFILE.EXT and place into that file all console or printer output from the next program. When the program is completed, console or printer output automatically returns to the normal mode. The third and fourth forms of the command can be given to terminate the operation prematurely.

When the option NO ECHO is included, console output will not appear at the console and printer output will not appear at the printer. The FILTER option changes each control character to two printable characters—a ^ symbol and the corresponding letter.

Normally only the output from an executing program is written to the disk file. However, with the SYSTEM option all output, including the command line, appears in the file.

The expression OUTPUT TO may be omitted from the PUT command.

RENAME	Rename a disk file
	(Built-in command and RENAME.COM extension)

FORMAT:

> RENAME
> RENAME PNAME2.EXT = PNAME1.EXT
> RENAME ambig2 = ambig1

DESCRIPTION:

The RENAME command changes the name of a disk file. Only the name in the directory is changed; the file itself is not altered. The ambiguous ? and * symbols may be used, but they must occur in identical positions in both names.

USE:

If the file is not on the default drive, include the drive name in either or both file names. If the parameters are omitted, RENAME will ask for them.

See chapter 3 for further details.

RMAC™	Macroassembler for assembly language programming
	(RMAC.COM transient)

FORMAT:

RMAC PNAME
RMAC PNAME $options

DESCRIPTION:

The relocatable macroassembler RMAC creates three new files from an assembly language source program and an optional macro library. The source program has a file type of ASM, and the macro library has a type LIB. The assembled code is located in a REL file, the symbol table is found in a SYM file, and the printer listing is a PRN file. The separate program LINK creates an executable file from the REL file.

USE:

A dollar sign rather than the usual square bracket precedes the options. A space must precede the dollar sign. If no options are given, all files are referenced to the default drive. You can select any other drive by using the appropriate options. See a macroassembler manual for more details. Also see MAC, LINK.

SAVE	Save contents of memory in a disk file
	(SAVE.COM transient)

FORMAT:

SAVE

DESCRIPTION:

The SAVE command creates a disk file from the contents of a selected portion of memory. This is usually the memory region starting at the address 100 hex; however, it may be anywhere. The memory image must be previously created by another program.

USE:

Execute SAVE (without a parameter) before creating the memory image. SAVE relocates itself into high memory and returns to CP/M. Run the program that creates the memory image you want to save. At the end of the program control returns to the CP/M system, and the SAVE program automatically takes over. SAVE then asks for the name of the new disk file and the starting and ending addresses of the memory to be saved. If a disk file of the same name already exists, you are asked for permission to delete it.

This program is used primarily by programmers.

SET	*Change file attributes, assign a label to a disk, set up password protection, and select the type of time and date tagging*
	(SET.COM transient program)

FORMAT:

    SET PNAME.EXT[option]
    SET ambig[option]
    SET D:[option]
    SET[option]

DESCRIPTION:

SET is used for several purposes. The most important application is changing the attributes read only or read/write and system or directory for a single file or a group of files. In addition, an entire disk drive can be set to read only or read/write status. The archive bit can also be changed.

A name or label and a separate password can be assigned to each disk and a password assigned to each individual file on the disk to keep unauthorized users from having access to these disk files. Both label and password follow the rules for file names. That is, the primary name can have as many as eight characters, and an optional extension can have up to three characters. The disk name can be displayed with SHOW.

A third capability of SET is selecting the type of time and date tagging. CP/M can encode two separate times and dates for each file. One of these refers to the date of last alteration, and the other is chosen to be either the creation date or the last access date. The separate program INITDIR formats a directory for time and date tagging, but SET is used to select the mode.

USE:

See Chapter 3 for a description of how to use SET to change the attributes for an individual file or a group of files. In this section we will look at the uses of SET that are not discussed in Chapter 3.

The archive attribute is used with PIP to make backup copies of altered files. PIP automatically sets the archive bit when the A option is given (see PIP). The archive bit can be changed with SET. The options are [ARCHIVE = ON] and [ARCHIVE = OFF].

A symbolic label is assigned with the NAME option. The label follows the rules for naming a disk file. For example, the command:

    SET B:[NAME = MYDISK]

assigns the label MYDISK to drive B. The label is encoded into the directory of the disk.

After a disk label has been assigned, it is possible to assign a password to the disk with the PASSWORD option. For example, the command:

    SET[PASSWORD = HIDDEN]

assigns the password HIDDEN to the disk. Password protection must be separately activated with the PROTECT option. The commands:

    SET[PROTECT = ON]
    SET[PROTECT = OFF]

turn password protection on and off. Passwords can also be assigned to individual disk files by including a file name parameter with the PASSWORD option.

There are four different password modes. For example, each of the following commands:

    SET PNAME.EXT[PROTECT = READ]
    SET PNAME.EXT[PROTECT = WRITE]
    SET PNAME.EXT[PROTECT = DELETE]
    SET PNAME.EXT[PROTECT = NONE]

sets one of the four modes for the disk file named PNAME.EXT. When the READ option is set, the password is required for reading, altering, copying, renaming, or deleting the file. This is the default mode. If the WRITE mode is set, a password is not necessary to read or copy a file, but it is needed to alter, rename, or delete the file. When DELETE mode is set, a password is needed to delete or rename a file. The password is not needed after the NONE option is chosen.

To use date and time tagging, you must first prepare the disk directory with INITDIR and set the system clock with DATE. Then two of three modes must be activated. Give the command:

```
SET[UPDATE = ON]
```

and then one of the two following commands:

```
SET[CREATE = ON]
SET[ACCESS = ON]
```

The UPDATE mode shows the date and time that a file was created with the editor or copied from another disk with PIP. The ACCESS mode shows when the file was last referenced. This includes inspecting with TYPE, making a copy to another disk with PIP, and executing a program. Since CREATE is like UPDATE, it is most useful to select the UPDATE and ACCESS options. Execute DIR with the FULL option to see the dates and times. After time and date tagging has been enabled, the DIR command with the [FULL] option will show the corresponding times and dates. See the DATE and INITDIR commands.

The archive flag is automatically turned off by the system editor when a file is altered. The flag is turned on when a file is copied by PIP using the A option. However, you may also change this flag with SET. The commands are:

```
SET ambig[ARCHIVE = ON]
SET ambig[ARCHIVE = OFF]
```

(ARCHIVE may be abbreviated to AR.)

SETDEF	Define or display disk search path and turn paging on or off
	(SETDEF.COM transient program)

FORMAT:

SETDEF
SETDEF D:
SETDEF[option]

DESCRIPTION:

You execute a transient program by typing its name. If the program is located on the current drive, you may omit the drive name. However, if it is on a different drive, you normally include the drive name with the file name so that CP/M can locate the program.

If you always work on drive B but execute programs located on drive A, you can redefine the way CP/M looks for a file. For example, CP/M can look for a file on drive A first, then on drive D, and finally on the current drive. This is called a search path.

USE:

Give the command SETDEF without a parameter to display the current search path. The search path can be changed by including the drive names separated by commas. An asterisk defines the current drive. For example, the command:

SETDEF A:, *

forces CP/M to first search drive A for a file to be executed. If CP/M cannot find the file on this drive, it looks on the current drive.

No drive name parameter is included when you use the options DISPLAY, NO DISPLAY, PAGE, and NO PAGE.

The DISPLAY option of SETDEF directs CP/M to show the file name and location of programs when they are executed. The NO DISPLAY option turns this feature off.

Programs such as TYPE and DIR display a page of 24 lines on the video screen and then stop until you press the carriage return or another key. Then the next screen is displayed. You can disable this feature with the [NO PAGE] option of SETDEF so that console output appears continuously. This mode is useful for quickly scanning the output or for sending the output to the printer.

The [PAGE] option reverses the effect of the [NO PAGE] option. The page length is changed with the DEVICE command.

See Chapter 3 for further explanation.

SHOW	Show characteristics of a disk
	(SHOW.COM transient program)

FORMAT:

SHOW[option]
SHOW D:[option]

DESCRIPTION:

The program SHOW displays the characteristics of an entire disk, in contrast to DIR, which displays the statistics of individual files. The SHOW information includes the remaining disk space; the remaining directory entries; the current user number; the numbers of the active user areas; and the disk drive characteristics such as capacity, block size, sector size, and sectors per track. The symbolic name assigned to the disk with SET can also be displayed.

USE:

SHOW executed without a parameter gives the remaining disk space for all logged-in drives and identifies the drives as read only or read/write. With a parameter, SHOW gives the information for the indicated drive.

The option parameter [DIR] gives the number of remaining directory entries. (This information can also be obtained from the separate program DIR.) The [USERS] option identifies the current user number as well as all active user areas and the number of files associated with each user.

The [DRIVE] option lists the physical features of the specified drive—storage capacity, number of directory entries, and block size. The [LABEL] option identifies the assigned symbolic name for the disk. The name is encoded in the directory with the SET command. This is useful for removable media like floppy disks.

See Chapter 3 for further details.

SID™	Debugger program to load, alter, and test assembly language programs
	(SID.COM transient program)

FORMAT:

    SID
    SID PNAME.EXT
    SID PNAME.EXT PNAME.SYM

DESCRIPTION:

SID (which stands for symbolic instruction debugger) is useful for assembly language programmers. It is used to develop programs assembled with MAC and RMAC. Executable COM or HEX files can be loaded with their symbol tables and run under precise control of SID. SID can disassemble executable code into its equivalent Intel 8080 mnemonics.

For additional information, refer to the CP/M SID manual supplied by Digital Research, Inc.

SUBMIT	*Execute commands from a disk file*
	(SUBMIT.COM transient program)

FORMAT:

    SUBMIT
    SUBMIT PNAME
    SUBMIT PNAME PARAM1 PARAM2 PARAM3 . . .

DESCRIPTION:

A sequence of commands normally given to CP/M from the console can be placed into a disk file and processed by SUBMIT instead. Input to an executing program can also be included. Then CP/M executes each line of the file as though it had been entered from the keyboard. When the list of commands has been exhausted, control returns to the console. This operation is known as batch processing.

The operation can be made more versatile by adding dummy parameters to the file. Then one batch file can perform several slightly different tasks.

USE:

You use the system editor to create a disk file containing the list of commands. The file type must be SUB. If the file name is PROFILE. SUB, CP/M Plus will automatically execute the commands in the file each time the computer is turned on.

Each line of the SUB is normally a CP/M command. However, when you include input to an executing program, the line begins with the < symbol. For example, the four lines:

    PIP
    <B: = A: * .TXT[VA]
    <B: = A: * .BAS[VA]
    <

will execute PIP and then make archival backup copies of all TXT and BAS files.

Slightly different tasks can be performed with the same SUB file when dummy parameters are placed in the file. The dummy parameters are named $1, $2, and $3, as needed. For example, suppose the file SMALL.SUB contains these lines:

```
DIR $1.*
PIP $2: = $1.BAK
ERASE $1.BAK
```

The command:

```
SUBMIT SMALL PROG B
```

directs SUBMIT to prepare the commands in the file SMALL.SUB for execution. Furthermore, the parameter PROG replaces the dummy parameter $1 and the parameter B replaces $2. Consequently, the following commands are issued to CP/M:

```
DIR PROG.*
PIP B: = PROG.BAK
ERASE PROG.BAK
```

For further explanation, see Chapter 3.

TYPE	*Display a text file on the console*
	(Built-in command and TYPE.COM extension)

FORMAT:

    TYPE
    TYPE PNAME.EXT
    TYPE ambig
    TYPE PNAME.EXT[NO PAGE]
    TYPE ambig[NO PAGE]

DESCRIPTION:

The TYPE command displays the contents of an individual text file or a collection of files on the console. The display stops each time the screen fills, though this feature can be disabled with the [NO PAGE] option.

USE:

The built-in version of TYPE can be executed from any disk and user area. The display freezes when the screen fills. Press the carriage return to see the next screenful or ^C to terminate the command prematurely. Use ^S and ^Q to freeze the screen and resume scrolling, respectively.

Obtain a complete printed listing by pressing ^P before giving the carriage return to the command. You can restrict the area of the listing by freezing the display with ^S at the appropriate place. Type ^P to engage the printer, then resume scrolling with ^Q. When listing a file on the printer, give the [NO PAGE] option so that the listing will not stop after each screen has been displayed.

The transient extension TYPE.COM is required if:

1. The option parameter is included
2. Ambiguous characters ? or * appear in the file name

3. The TYPE command is given without a parameter

4. More than one file-name parameter is given

If you have not established a search path with SETDEF, you must include the drive location for the TYPE.COM file. You must not use TYPE to display COM or REL files.

USER	*Change current user area*
	(Built-in command)

FORMAT:

USER
USER n

DESCRIPTION:

Each disk can be divided into as many as 16 different user areas, numbered 0 to 15. By this means, different working areas can be isolated from each other, though system files in user area 0 are available to all user areas.

User area 0 is automatically selected when CP/M is started. The built-in command USER changes the user area to the area specified.

USE:

If you execute USER without a parameter, CP/M will ask for one. Alternatively, you can include the parameter with the command. When the user number is not 0, it is identified in the prompt. The active user areas can be determined with the transient program SHOW.

See Chapter 3 for more details.

XREF	*Cross reference listing for assembler*
	(XREF.COM transient program)

FORMAT:

>XREF PNAME
>XREF PNAME $P

DESCRIPTION:

The assemblers MAC and RMAC create an alphabetical listing of all symbols and their assigned values. XREF provides additional information by creating a cross-reference listing of these symbols. Each time a symbol is referenced, the corresponding line number is given. The PRN and SYM files from the assembler are used to create an XRF file.

USE:

Normally, the XRF file is written to disk. However, the P option sends the listing to the printer. When only a single reference is given, it indicates that a symbol was defined but never used.

Notice that the option parameter is preceded by a dollar sign rather than the usual square bracket. A space must precede the dollar sign.

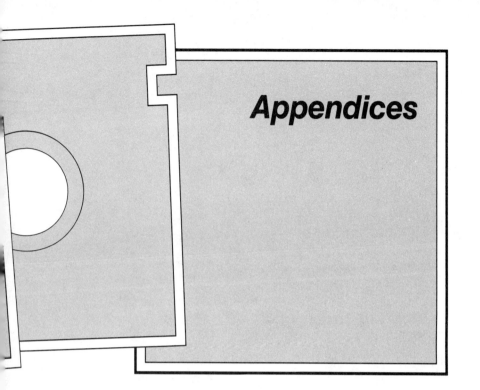

Appendices

APPENDIX A
CP/M PLUS AND CP/M VERSION 2 COMPARED

CP/M Plus, also known as CP/M version 3, shares many features with the previous version 2 (which includes versions 2.0 and 2.2). The earlier versions, 1.3 and 1.4, are so different that many programs designed to run on them will not run with versions 2 and CP/M Plus. In the same way, programs designed for version 2 and CP/M Plus cannot be expected to run on versions 1.3 and 1.4. Both version 2 and CP/M Plus contain the console command processor (CCP), the basic input-output system (BIOS), and the basic disk operating system (BDOS) modules (see Chapter 6). Furthermore, most programs written for version 2 will also run on version 3 without alteration. Following is a brief summary of the new features. Other details are mentioned throughout the book as they are relevant.

MEMORY

CP/M Plus can be implemented with 64K bytes of memory. This nonbanked configuration closely resembles version 2. However, CP/M Plus is more commonly provided as a bank-switched version with three switchable banks and one fixed bank. The fixed bank and one of the switchable banks combine to produce 64K bytes of memory. Memory layout for the two methods is diagrammed in Figures 6.2 and 6.3 of Chapter 6.

With the banked version the BIOS and BDOS are split into two parts. A small portion of the BIOS and BDOS reside in the common fixed memory that is always accessible, and the remainder resides in bank 0. Bank 1 and a portion of the fixed memory are allocated to the transient program area (TPA), where transient programs are executed. The working copy of the CCP also runs here. Bank 3 contains disk buffers and a duplicate copy of the CCP.

FUNCTIONAL MODULES

The CCP for version 2 is located at the top of the TPA and can be overwritten by a program when space is needed. Both the CCP and the BDOS are reloaded from the system tracks of disk A at the next warm start. By contrast, the CCP for CP/M Plus is located at the beginning of the TPA and is always overwritten by an executing program. As with version 2, the CCP is reloaded at the next warm start. However, the BDOS is not reloaded at this time. For the bank-switched version, the CCP can be restored from a duplicate copy kept in bank 0 or 2. This obviates a disk access when a warm start is performed, greatly speeding up the operation.

A copy of the BIOS and BDOS for version 2 is located on the system tracks of disk A. By contrast, the BIOS and BDOS for CP/M Plus are located in the data area of the disk as a regular CP/M file, named CPM3.SYS. This file is not loaded at each warm start, but only when CP/M Plus is first started up. A copy of the CCP is usually located on the system tracks of the disk as it is with version 2. However, for some computers the CCP is a regular COM file located in the data area of the disk.

Nearly all of the BDOS functions of version 2 are incorporated into CP/M Plus. An exception is the IOBYTE operations. (The IOBYTE is used in versions 1 and 2 to change peripheral assignments. This task is performed in CP/M Plus with DEVICE, PUT, and GET.) An additional complication occurs with the banked version because the major portion of the BIOS is not present during program execution. Therefore, direct BIOS calls cannot be performed. However, transient programs can access the BIOS indirectly through a BDOS call designed for this purpose.

BUILT-IN AND TRANSIENT COMMANDS

Five of the six built-in CP/M Plus commands—DIR, ERASE, RENAME, TYPE, and USER—are similar to the built-in commands of version 2. DIRSYS is a new command. The DIRSYS command can be abbreviated to four letters, and the others can be reduced to three letters. Four of the commands—DIR, ERASE, RENAME, and TYPE—are paired with transient versions of the same name, which are automatically executed when additional features are requested. Transients were not provided with earlier versions.

The useful STAT program of version 2 is not provided. Its features are divided among the programs DIR, SET, SHOW, and DEVICE.

SUBMIT has two new features in CP/M Plus. The program XSUB was used with SUBMIT in version 2 to allow input from executing programs. This feature has been incorporated into the CP/M Plus version of SUBMIT. Second, each time CP/M Plus is started up, it looks for a submit file named PROFILE. If such a file exists, CP/M executes the commands it finds there. By this means general housekeeping tasks can be performed automatically on startup.

In CP/M Plus PIP can copy programs from the current user area into any other user area. PIP also reproduces the read-only and system attributes when a single file is copied. This feature was not available in version 2. A new archive attribute is incorporated. PIP can be directed to copy only those files that have not been previously copied. It then sets the archive feature of the copied files so they will not be copied again later.

The PUT program of CP/M Plus alters CP/M so that console and printer output can also go to a disk file. Alternatively, console output can be sent to the printer. In a similar way, GET directs CP/M Plus to read console input from a disk file rather than from the keyboard.

SAVE, which was a built-in program in version 2, is a separate transient program in CP/M Plus. When it is executed, it relocates itself at the top of the TPA. After the next program has completed, it is automatically reactivated. You can then save any portion of memory to disk.

In CP/M Plus you can establish an automatic file-search path with SETDEF. CP/M can thereby be directed to first search drive A for a transient program even though drive B might be the current drive.

CP/M Plus programs such as PIP can be prematurely terminated with ^C. It is not possible to prematurely terminate CP/M version 2 programs.

Parameters omitted from CP/M Plus commands are automatically requested. The ambiguous ? and * symbols can be used in the RENAME command. This was not possible in version 2.

As with version 2, the current drive letter is displayed in the prompt. In addition, the user number is shown if it is not 0. The current drive is changed by giving the new letter followed by a colon.

Several mechanisms make the operation of user areas more convenient. Any system file in user area 0 is accessible to any other user area of the disk. The user number can also be changed in the same way as the drive. For example, the command 2B: changes to user area 2 on drive B.

EDITING

A powerful feature of the banked version of CP/M Plus allows editing of the command line. This feature is not provided with earlier versions. The cursor can be moved both left and right without destroying the text. In this way characters can be inserted and deleted. The previous command line can be recalled and executed again exactly as before, or it can be edited before being executed again. More than one statement can be given on a single command line if the commands are separated by an exclamation mark. As text scrolls on the video screen, CP/M Plus will stop the display at each screenful. Pressing the carriage return will display the next screen. Scrolling can also be stopped by ^S and resumed with ^Q.

DISK DIRECTORY

As with earlier versions, each disk contains a directory that lists the names and locations of files stored on the disk. However, CP/M Plus can create additional directory entries for keeping track of two values of time and date for each file. In addition, a symbolic name and password can be assigned to each disk, and a separate password can be given to each disk file.

The CP/M directory entries are not arranged in any particular order. In earlier versions CP/M locates a file simply by looking at each directory entry one after the other until the name is found. When there are many file names in the directory, it may take a relatively long time to find a particular name. The situation corresponds to a directory for an office building that is arranged randomly rather than alphabetically.

File names are also listed randomly in the CP/M Plus disk directory. However, CP/M Plus creates a separate index to the directory that greatly speeds up the search for a particular file. The encoding scheme, known as *hashing*, serves the same purpose as arranging a building directory in alphabetical order. The hashing table is placed in memory bank 0 or 2.

Another feature that greatly speeds up the operation of CP/M PLUS is called *least recently used (LRU)* buffering. Each time a new disk sector is read, a copy is placed into a spare memory bank. When a disk sector is needed, CP/M first looks in the LRU buffer to see if it already has a copy. If so, a copy is taken from there rather than from the disk. When the LRU buffer is filled, the least recently used sector is overwritten with the next sector that is read.

CP/M Plus does not require a warm start or a resetting of the disks after a disk has been changed. When CP/M detects a disk change during a write operation, the new disk is automatically logged in. Both the maximum file size and the maximum disk size have been increased with CP/M Plus. Individual files may be as large as 32 megabytes and disks may be as large as 512 megabytes. Blocking and deblocking routines are not needed in the BIOS since the BDOS can read a complete sector of any size.

FILE TRANSFER

With previous versions of CP/M, it was necessary to write a different version of a file transfer program for each different computer. However, the BIOS and BDOS of CP/M Plus incorporate entries for determining auxiliary input and output status. Thus, a single version of a file-transfer program can run on any CP/M Plus computer.

APPENDIX B
PRACTICAL HINTS

INTRODUCTION

Although a computer is a complex machine that must be treated with respect, if you follow some simple procedures and precautions you should be able to make the best use of your computer and avoid problems. This appendix presents two kinds of information: practical techniques for using and caring for your hardware, and hints for using the operations most effectively. For more detailed information about computer care, a good source is *Don't! (or How to Care for Your Computer)* by Rodnay Zaks (SYBEX, 1981).

THE WORKSPACE

Keeping your computer workspace organized will make it easier for you to use the computer and avoid problems. Make sure all necessary documentation, blank disks, computer programs, and other supplies are available. Keep a listing of the steps needed to start up the computer and the necessary precautions close at hand. Figure B.1 presents a typical list of supplies.

FLOPPY DISKS

Always treat your floppy disks carefully, as they are easily damaged. Floppy disks are magnetic media. Therefore, do not place them near a magnetic field or a steel object that might be magnetized. Magnetic fields can be produced by transformers, telephones, screwdrivers, steel desks, and any other steel objects. When traveling by air, do not place disks in your luggage. Hand carry them and be sure to ask for a separate inspection when you board the plane. Do not let the disks be X-rayed, since the machine creates a magnetic field.

Checklist for starting computer
New floppy disks
Printer paper
Envelopes
Printer ribbon
Printwheels
System disk
Disk for applications programs
Computer manual
Printer manual
Video screen manual
Applications program manual

Figure B.1 – Supplies for the Computer

Always place disks in their envelopes when you are not using them. Do not expose them to a dusty or smoky environment. Special care must be taken in a dry climate, as disks can accumulate a static charge that makes dust and other particles stick to the surface. Do not scratch, touch, or attempt to clean the disk surface or open the outer cover.

You should always have a label on each disk, indicating the date and the contents. Never write on a disk with a pen, pencil, or sharp object; the pressure can damage the surface. Instead, use a felt-tipped pen or write on the label and then affix it to the disk. Use only the labels that are provided with a box of disks. The wrong kind of label can damage the disk or the disk drive.

Do not bend, fold, spindle, or mutilate disks. Do not expose them to heat or direct sunlight. Remove all disks before turning off the computer.

Try to prevent the buildup of static electricity in your computer room. A special antistatic spray may be used on carpeting. The most effective solution is a humidifier.

THE PRINTER

Computer printers will work very reliably for months or even years without needing attention if they are treated with care. All mechanical adjustments must be correct, without exception, or the printer may not operate correctly.

An example of an adjustment that should be checked is the paper thickness lever. If you use thin paper when the lever is set for thick, the printer may malfunction in an unpredictable manner. There may appear to be a software problem, whereas only a simple adjustment is necessary. Other settings on the printer control full or half duplex, online or local, single or double line feed, baud rate, parity, and word length. Read the manufacturer's instructions for your printer so you can understand what these settings do and how to reset them if the switches are changed.

Because printers usually run quite slowly, you may be tempted to walk away from the computer while a listing is in progress. Be sure you check on the operation frequently to see that everything is in order. This is especially important at the beginning of a listing, because the paper might jam in the printer. The operator should always be present when printing adhesive labels, as labels are more likely to cause jamming than regular paper. This will require restarting the operation, and it could also damage the printer.

Printer ribbons may be either carbon or cloth. All carbon ribbons and some cloth ribbons move in only one direction. However, some cloth ribbons occasionally reverse direction. At the moment of reversal the characters tend to be printed too lightly or not at all.

Whenever a problem occurs during printing, the listing will have to be restarted. If the first part is all right, it may be possible to restart the listing at the place where the problem occurs. Word processors such as WordStar have provisions for this. If you are printing a file with PIP, you can use the S option to start a file in the middle. If a file is short, it is easier to restart the listing from the beginning.

If the printer does not work when the system is turned on, check all printer settings. In particular, check that the online/local switch is set to online. If you use different versions of CP/M from time to time, verify that your CP/M disk corresponds correctly to the type of printer. This is a common mistake.

DISK FILES

Initial Precautions

Be sure to format a new disk before you use it for the first time. Always make a backup copy of any new program or disk before it is first used. Then put the original away in a safe place. During a long editing session, frequently save the edit buffer in case of a power failure or human error. In addition, frequently make a backup copy onto another disk.

Each disk envelope should contain a printed listing of the disk contents. Make the listing by engaging the printer with ^P and then executing DIR with the [FULL] option.

Keep a backup copy of any important disks in a separate location so that you do not risk losing all your information at once. If you have an office computer, keep the backup disks at home. If you have a home computer, keep the backups at the office.

Size

There is a limit to the useful storage capacity of each disk as well as the available number of directory entries. As more and more files are saved on a disk, the free space can become exhausted. Another problem can arise if a single file is larger than the capacity of the disk. For fastest editing and duplication file size should be limited to the available memory. This is about 40–50K bytes. For example, you can keep each chapter of a book as a separate file rather than making the entire book into one file. It is more difficult to break a data file, such as a list of customer names, into several parts. One solution is to arrange a list in alphabetical order. Then you can break it into several parts—A–L and M–Z for example—on separate disks.

Before you edit a file, determine the file size with the [SIZE] or [FULL] option of DIR. Also determine the remaining disk space with SHOW. If you want to place the edited file on the same disk as the original, there must be sufficient room. In fact, the remaining space on the disk should be more than the size of the original file because the editor may need some work space. For example, if the file to be edited contains 80K bytes, the disk should contain 120K bytes of free space in addition to the original file. If there is not enough space, you can place the edited file on a different disk from the original file.

Sorting large files can also be a problem. You will need to have room for the sorted version as well as the original. One type of sorting routine loads the entire file into main memory, which limits your file to 40K or 50K bytes. However, a different sorting program, such as SuperSort™ by MicroPro, can sort very large files from disk to disk.

System Files

Part of the CP/M Plus system resides on the system tracks of drive A. This is a region of the disk that is not normally accessible. Therefore, program storage space is not reduced by the presence of CP/M on the system tracks. However, there are additional parts to CP/M Plus.

The disk file named CPM3.SYS must reside in the data area of drive A. Also, for some versions of CP/M Plus a second disk file, named CCP.COM, must also be present on drive A. These files should have the system attribute set so that they will not show in normal DIR listings. You can give the DIRSYS command or the DIR command with the [SYS] option to see that they are present.

It is not necessary to place CP/M on the system tracks of disks that are used only in drives other than A, though it does no harm. The system files CPM3.SYS and CCP.COM can also be placed on disks that are used in other drives. In this case some file storage space is lost because they reside in the data area. If the storage capacity of your floppy disks is large enough, it is a good idea to place these routines on all disks. Then any disk can be used in drive A. On the other hand, if your disks have a small capacity, you may not want to lose the storage space. Disks without these files can be used in drive A if you do not perform a cold boot.

Editing

If you need to change a single word or expression throughout the file, the substitution command of your editor can accomplish this conveniently (See Chapter 5 for details). You can also use the substitution command to incorporate a complicated expression that is needed at many places in a report. Let us see how to do this.

Suppose, for example, that the chemical compound naphthalene is mentioned 30 times in a report. At each point enter a symbol such as P$ instead. Then after the document is finished, use the substitution command to change each occurrence of P$ to naphthalene.

Another way to enter complicated expressions is with programmable function keys, if you have these on your console. See the manufacturer's directions.

Executing a Sequence of Commands

You can easily execute a lengthy sequence of commands or a frequently used set of commands by creating a disk file of the commands and running SUBMIT. See chapters 3 and 7 for more details.

Printing Multiple Files

There are a number of ways to print multiple files. You can create a SUBMIT file, called PRINT.SUB for example, to print several files with one command. Another method is to engage the printer with ^P and give an ambiguous file name to the TYPE command. Be sure to include the [NO PAGE] option so the listing does not stop at each page.

Damaged Files

A disk file can become unusable or damaged because of operator error, a system malfunction, or power failure. A transient program may no longer execute, or it may not be possible to edit or list a text file. If you have a backup copy of the file, delete the damaged version and make a new copy from the backup. If you do not have a backup copy, you should try to recover as much of a text file as possible. You are not likely to succeed with a transient program, but it may be possible to recover almost all of a text file.

There are several commercial programs for recovering damaged files. Some require extensive knowledge of assembly language programming and a familiarity with the CP/M operating system. Others are very easy to use. Two of the best and easiest to use are BADLIM™ and FILEFIX.

Damage to the Disk Surface

Each sector of information stored on a disk has a cyclical redundancy code (CRC) formed from the contents of the sector. When the computer reads each sector, it recomputes the CRC and compares the information to the recorded CRC value. If the two do not agree, it means that there is a bad sector and the information is likely to be incorrect.

The surface of the disk can be damaged in one of two ways. A region can be incorrectly magnetized, or there can be a defect such as a scratch in the surface. It may be possible to correct a magnetic fault with FORMAT. However, if the surface is damaged, the disk usually must be discarded.

If a bad sector occurs in the data region of the disk, programs such as BADLIM can isolate the bad sector so that the computer will not use this region of the disk again. However, if the bad sector is located in the directory region, the disk is unusuable. If you can isolate the damaged sector with BADLIM, you may be able to use ERASE, rather than FORMAT, to repair the surface. Otherwise, the disk must be discarded.

Erasing a Disk

You may need to erase a disk for one of two reasons:

- The programs are no longer needed.
- The disk surface is damaged.

For the first case give the SHOW command with the [USERS] option to see if there are any other active user areas. Also give the DIRSYS command to see if there are system files. If no other user areas are active and there are no system files, then you can erase all files with the command ERASE *.*. Otherwise, it may be easier to execute FORMAT or COPY, as described in Chapter 2.

TERMINATING EXECUTION

If you accidently execute the wrong program or execute a program with the wrong parameters, it may be possible to terminate execution (that is, stop the program before it finishes) by typing a ^C. This should work for all CP/M system programs such as TYPE or PIP. However, it may not be possible to terminate programs from other suppliers in this way. In this case you can interrupt execution with the reset switch. Do not turn off the computer or remove disks while a program is executing and the disks are running, or you may damage the disks.

THE SEVEN COMMANDMENTS FOR RECOVERY FROM SYSTEM FAILURE

Suspect the Operator First:

1. Check the mechanical items:

   • Are all switch positions correct? Check systematically, with no exceptions.

   • Are fuses intact?

   • Are all cables attached, with no loose connections?

   • Are all cables in the correct place?

2. Did you give the correct command?

   • Remove disks and turn everything off. Turn the system on.

   • Repeat the command.

Suspect the Disk Next:

3. Use a fresh disk. The current disk may have been damaged through incorrect handling and will cause erratic behavior.

- Use a backup disk. Do not use any program on your current disk.
- If no complete single backup exists, take the time to make one.

Suspect the Software:

4. Make sure that you are using the correct programs:

- The correct CP/M version if you have several
- The correct transient program for your application
- The correct application program

Many application programs, word processors in particular, must be adapted to your terminal and printer. Otherwise, some keys on the terminal may not work, and you may not be able to print a file.

Suspect the Hardware Last:

5. Check the mechanicals again, very thoroughly.

- In particular, remove boards, clean the connections with an eraser, and insert them back in place.
- If the source of the malfunction can be attributed to a board, remove components from sockets, clean connections, and reinsert them.

6. Try to identify a suspected malfunctioning device by exchanging it with a known good one: swap boards, console, and printer. This will give you positive proof and save much time. Never suspect a device until you have tried swapping it with a known good one. Otherwise, a good deal of effort could be wasted.

7. From now on, use the correct prevention techniques, as explained in this book.

APPENDIX C
THE CP/M CONTROL CHARACTERS

COMMAND	ACTION
^A	Move cursor one characte
^B	Move cursor to beginning line if cursor is already at
^C	Terminate CP/M program
^E	Move cursor to next line (
^F	Move cursor one characte
^G	Delete character at curso
^H	Delete character to left of
^I	Move cursor to next tab p
^J	Execute command (line fe
^K	Delete from cursor to en
^M	Execute command (carri
^P	Engage or disengage prin
^Q	Resume scrolling after ^
^R	Redisplay line
^S	Freeze screen
^U	Delete all characters in li
^W	Recall previous comman
^X	Delete all characters to l
^Z	Mark end of string in PIP

*Indicates commands that apply only to the ba

APPENDIX D
ASCII CHARACTER SET

CODE	CHAR	CODE	CHAR	CODE	CHAR	CODE	CHAR
00	NUL	20[1]		40	@	60[5]	`
01	SOH	21	!	41	A	61	a
02	STX	22	"	42	B	62	b
03	ETX	23	#	43	C	63	c
04	EOT	24	$	44	D	64	d
05	ENQ	25	%	45	E	65	e
06	ACK	26	&	46	F	66	f
07	BEL	27[2]	'	47	G	67	g
08	BS	28	(	48	H	68	h
09	TAB	29	)	49	I	69	i
0A	LF	2A	*	4A	J	6A	j
0B	VT	2B	+	4B	K	6B	k
0C	FF	2C[3]	,	4C	L	6C	l
0D	CR	2D	−	4D	M	6D	m
0E	SO	2E	.	4E	N	6E	n
0F	SI	2F	/	4F	O	6F	o
10	DLE	30	0	50	P	70	p
11	DC1	31	1	51	Q	71	q
12	DC2	32	2	52	R	72	r
13	DC3	33	3	53	S	73	s
14	DC4	34	4	54	T	74	t
15	NAK	35	5	55	U	75	u
16	SYN	36	6	56	V	76	v
17	ETB	37	7	57	W	77	w
18	CAN	38	8	58	X	78	x
19	EM	39	9	59	Y	79	y
1A	SUB	3A	:	5A	Z	7A	z
1B	ESC	3B	;	5B	[	7B	{
1C	FS	3C	<	5C	\	7C	|
1D	GS	3D	=	5D	]	7D[6]	}
1E	RS	3E	>	5E	↑	7E	~
1F	US	3F	?	5F[4]	←	7F[7]	RUBOUT

[1] space [3] comma [5] accent mark [7] or DEL
[2] single quote [4] or underline [6] or ALT MODE

Index

Ambiguous file name, 42, 63, 94, 97
Applications software, 6
Archive flag (*see* PIP and DIR)
Argument (*see* parameter)
Attributes
   changing, 72
   determining, 60
   file, 60
Automatic startup, 78
AUX: (*see* peripheral device)

Backspace character, 25
Bank-switched memory, 150
Basic disk operating system
   (BDOS), 150
Basic input-output system (BIOS), 165
Batch processing of commands
   (*see* SUBMIT)
BDOS, 150
   call to create a disk file, 165
   call to open a disk file, 158
   function calls, 159
   program interaction with, 158
BIOS, 165
Block, disk, 28
   size, 68
Boot
   cold, 12
   warm, 24
Booting the system, 12

Bootstrap loader, 12
Buffer, edit, 112
Built-in commands, 39, 50
   abbreviations, 50
   DIR, 55–61
   TYPE, 53–54
   USER, 54–55
Byte, 3

Carriage return key, 12
CCP, 148–149
Central processing unit (CPU), 3
Cold start, 12
Colon, in device name, 35
Command
   built-in, 50
   transient, 50
Command file (*see* SUBMIT)
Command line, 48
   tail, 49
CON: (*see* peripheral device)
Concatenating files, 100–104
Console command processor
   (CCP), 148–149
Console device (*see* peripheral device)
Control characters, 21, 23
   editing with, 24
Control key, 23
COPY program, 29, 32, 97, 167

Copying
  CP/M with COPYSYS, 30
  disks (*see* PIP)
  system tracks, 30–32, 168
COPYSYS program, 30–32, 168
Correction of typing errors, 23, 25
CP/M
  BDOS, 150
  BIOS, 149
  CCP, 148
  comparison with CP/M Plus,
    225–229
  copying with COPYSYS, 30
  memory allocation, 150
  organization of, 147–164
  TPA, 151
CPU, 3
Cursor, 20

DATE, 170
Date stamping, 30, 71
Default drive, changing, 50
Deleting a file, 64–65, 183
DEVICE, 81–84, 172
  changing peripheral assignments,
    81
  sending to more than one, 83
  (*see also* peripheral device)
Device
  assignments, 81–84, 172
  names, 81
DIR, 39, 55–61, 174
  archive flag, 110
  determining file attributes, 60
  determining file size, 58
  file-name parameters, 56
  listing the directory, 55
  option parameters, 57
  transient extension, 57
Directory, disk, 39
  space, 70–72
DIRSYS program, 39, 61–62, 176
Disk, 5
  block, 28, 68
  care of, 9, 231

default, 20
directory, 39, 55
file, 6
file control block (FCB), 154
file name, 38
floppy, 56
formatting, 28
hard, 5
label, 73
log in, 69
organization, 152
partitioning into user areas, 111–112
password, 74
record, 68
remaining space, 68–70
resetting, 69
sector, 8
system, 28
system tracks, 30
track, 8
write protection, 8–9
Disk operating system, 6, 18, 28
Displaying a file, 36, 53
Dummy parameters, 78
DUMP program, 176
Duplicating a disk
  system disk, 30–32
  with COPY, 33
Duplicating a file with PIP, 32

ED program, 119–144, 178
  adding text, 135
  altering a file, 126
  altering text, 135
  combining commands, 133
  creating a file, 124
  deleting characters, 135
  displaying text, 131
  edit buffer, 122
  ending the edit session, 141
  error messages, 143
  free space, 134
  inserting a disk file, 137
  inserting characters, 135
  line numbers, 133

manipulating the character
    pointer, 128
moving a block of text, 138
repeating commands, 139
search and replace, 130, 137
source file, 122
temporary file, 142
Edit buffer, 122
Editing a line, 24
Editor, system, 34
End of file, 101
Enter key, 12
ERASE, 64–65, 183
    as option parameter, 65
Erasing
    a file, 64
    a line, 26
Extension, file-name, 40

FCB, 154
File, 6, 38
    binary, 53
    size, 58
    system, 55, 60
    text, 53, 101
File attributes, 60
    archive, 110
    changing with SET, 72
    determining with DIR, 60
    read-only, read/write, 60
    system, directory, 60
File control block, 154
File name, 38, 40
    ambiguous, 42, 63
    changing with RENAME, 62–64
    erasing, 64
    examples, 41
    extension, 40
    parameter, 49
    primary, 40
    type, 40
    valid characters, 42
File protection, 8–9
File-search path, 66, 95
Flag, archive, 110

Floppy disk, 5, 6
    care of, 9, 231
FORMAT program, 29, 185
Formatting a disk, 28
Freezing the video screen, 27
Function number, BDOS, 159–160

GENCOM program, 186
GET program, 187
Group (*see* block)

Hard copy, 4, 27
Hard disk, 5
Hardware, 2
HELP program, 188
HEXCOM program, 190

INITDIR program, 191

Kilobyte, 3

Label, disk, 73
LIB program, 192
Line numbers
    adding with PIP, 106
    with ED, 133
Line-feed character, 35
LINK program, 193
Logical device, 81
LST: (*see* peripheral device)

MAC program, 194
Mapping (*see* DEVICE)
Memory
    allocation, 150–151
    bank-switched, 150–151
    fixed, 151
    partitioning of, 151–152
    volatile, 5
Monitor, 4

NO PAGE option, 38, 53

Operating system, 6, 18, 28
Option parameter, 49, 115
  DIR, 57
  ERASE, 65
  PIP (*see* PIP)
  SET, 74
  SHOW, 70, 71, 74
  TYPE, 38

Parameter
  option (*see* option parameter)
  to command, 48
Parity bit, zeroing, 114
Password protection, 74–76
PATCH program, 195
Peripheral device, 2
  assignment (*see* DEVICE)
  AUX:, 81
  CON:, 34, 81, 95, 104
  LST:, 37, 81, 108
  PRN:, 109
  sending to two devices, 83
Physical device, 81
PIP program, 87–116, 196
  aborting an operation, 100
  adding line numbers, 106
  ambiguous symbols, 94
  archive flag, 110
  backing up a large disk, 110
  concatenating files, 100–104
  copying a complete disk, 97
  copying files, 89–100
    from disk to disk, 32, 89
    one file, 35
    portion of a file, 107
    read-only files, 112
    several files, 91–92
    system files, 112
    to another user area, 107
  creating a disk file, 95
  displaying text, 36, 105
  execution without a parameter, 91
    inserting characters, 103
    new user area, 111
  option parameters, 105–115

printing a file, 108
  transfer to peripheral device, 104
  verifying, 90
  zeroing the parity bit, 114
Primary name, 40
Printing a file
  with ^P, 27
  with PIP, 108
  with TYPE, 27
PRN: (*see* peripheral device)
Prompt, 20
PUT program, 204

Random access memory (RAM), 3
Read-only disk, 73
Read-only file, 112
Recalling previous command, 26
Record, disk, 68
RENAME command, 62–64, 205
Renaming a file, 62
  ambiguous symbols, 63
Resetting disks, 69
Return key, 12
RMAC program, 206

SAVE program, 207
Scrolling, 27
Search and replace (*see* ED program)
Sector, disk, 8
SET program, 72–76, 208
SET
  changing file attributes with, 72
  password protection, 74–76
  setting disk to read only with, 73
SETDEF program, 66–67, 211
  establishing a file-search path, 66
SHOW program, 68–72, 213
  determining active users, 70
  determining directory space, 71
  determining disk space, 68
SID program, 214
Software, 2
  applications, 6
  system, 5
Source file, 122

Starting up the computer, 11
String, 107 (*see* also ED program, search and replace)
SUBMIT program, 76–81, 215
  automatic start up, 78
  control characters, 80
  executing commands from a disk file, 76–77
  input to executing programs, 80
  parameters, 78
System disk, 28
  duplicating, 30–32
System editor, 34
System files, 55, 60, 112
  directory, 61
System tracks, 30
System software, 5

Text editor (*see* ED Program)
Text file, 53, 101
Time and date stamping, 30, 71
Time of day, 170
TPA, 151
Track, disk, 8
Tracks, system, 30
Transient command, 50
  DIR, 55–61
  DIRSYS, 61–62
  ERASE, 64–65
  RENAME, 62–64
  SET, 72–76

SHOW, 68–72
TYPE, 53–54
Transient program, 50
Transient program area, 50
Turning the computer on and off, 11–13
TYPE command, 36, 53–54, 217
  NO PAGE option, 38, 53
  transient extension, 38

User area
  active, 70
  changing, 54
  establishing new, 111–112
USER command, 54–55, 219

Video screen, 4
  cursor, 20
  displaying a file on, 36
  freezing, 27
Volatile memory, 5

Warm boot, 24
Wild card (*see* ambiguous file name)
Write protection, 8–9

XREF program, 220

., 97, 100

Selections from The SYBEX Library

Buyer's Guides

THE BEST OF TI 99/4A™ CARTRIDGES
by Thomas Blackadar
150 pp., illustr., Ref. 0-137
Save yourself time and frustration when buying TI 99/4A software. This buyer's guide gives an overview of the best available programs, with information on how to set up the computer to run them.

FAMILY COMPUTERS UNDER $200
by Doug Mosher
160 pp., illustr., Ref. 0-149
Find out what these inexpensive machines can do for you and your family. "If you're just getting started . . . this is the book to read before you buy."—Richard O'Reilly, Los Angeles newspaper columnist

PORTABLE COMPUTERS
by Sheldon Crop and Doug Mosher
128 pp., illustr., Ref. 0-144
"This book provides a clear and concise introduction to the expanding new world of personal computers."—Mark Powelson, Editor, *San Francisco Focus Magazine*

THE BEST OF VIC-20™ SOFTWARE
by Thomas Blackadar
150 pp., illustr., Ref. 0-139
Save yourself time and frustration with this buyer's guide to VIC-20 software. Find the best game, music, education, and home management programs on the market today.

SELECTING THE RIGHT DATA BASE SOFTWARE
SELECTING THE RIGHT WORD PROCESSING SOFTWARE
SELECTING THE RIGHT SPREADSHEET SOFTWARE
by Kathy McHugh and Veronica Corchado
80 pp., illustr., Ref. 0-174, 0-177, 0-178
This series on selecting the right business software offers the busy professional concise, informative reviews of the best available software packages.

Introduction to Computers

OVERCOMING COMPUTER FEAR
by Jeff Berner
112 pp., illustr., Ref. 0-145
This easy-going introduction to computers helps you separate the facts from the myths.

COMPUTER ABC'S
by Daniel Le Noury and Rodnay Zaks
64 pp., illustr., Ref. 0-167
This beautifully illustrated, colorful book for parents and children takes you alphabetically through the world of computers, explaining each concept in simple language.

PARENTS, KIDS, AND COMPUTERS
by Lynne Alper and Meg Holmberg
208 pp., illustr., Ref. 0-151
This book answers your questions about the educational possibilities of home computers.

THE COLLEGE STUDENT'S COMPUTER HANDBOOK
by Bryan Pfaffenberger
350 pp., illustr., Ref. 0-170
This friendly guide will aid students in selecting a computer system for college study, managing information in a college course, and writing research papers.

COMPUTER CRAZY
by Daniel Le Noury
100 pp., illustr., Ref. 0-173
No matter how you feel about computers, these cartoons will have you laughing about them.

DON'T!
(or How to Care for Your Computer)
by Rodnay Zaks
214pp., 100 illustr., Ref. 0-065
The correct way to handle and care for all elements of a computer system, including what to do when something doesn't work.

YOUR FIRST COMPUTER
by Rodnay Zaks
258 pp., 150 illustr., Ref. 0-045
The most popular introduction to small computers and their peripherals: what they do and how to buy one.

INTERNATIONAL MICROCOMPUTER DICTIONARY
120 pp., Ref. 0-067
All the definitions and acronyms of micro-computer jargon defined in a handy pocket-sized edition. Includes translations of the most popular terms into ten languages.

FROM CHIPS TO SYSTEMS: AN INTRODUCTION TO MICROPROCESSORS
by Rodnay Zaks
552 pp., 400 illustr., Ref. 0-063
A simple and comprehensive introduction

to microprocessors from both a hardware and software standpoint: what they are, how they operate, how to assemble them into a complete system.

Personal Computers

ATARI

YOUR FIRST ATARI® PROGRAM
by Rodnay Zaks
150 pp., illustr., Ref. 0-130
A fully illustrated, easy-to-use introduction to ATARI BASIC programming. Will have the reader programming in a matter of hours.

BASIC EXERCISES FOR THE ATARI®
by J.P. Lamoitier
251 pp., illustr., Ref. 0-101
Teaches ATARI BASIC through actual practice using graduated exercises drawn from everyday applications.

THE EASY GUIDE TO YOUR ATARI® 600XL/800XL
by Thomas Blackadar
175 pp., illustr., Ref. 0-125
This jargon-free companion will help you get started on the right foot with your new 600XL or 800XL ATARI computer.

ATARI® BASIC PROGRAMS IN MINUTES
by Stanley R. Trost
170 pp., illustr., Ref. 0-143
You can use this practical set of programs without any prior knowledge of BASIC! Application examples are taken from a wide variety of fields, including business, home management, and real estate.

Commodore 64/VIC-20

THE COMMODORE 64™/VIC-20™ BASIC HANDBOOK
by Douglas Hergert
144 pp., illustr., Ref. 0-116
A complete listing with descriptions and

instructive examples of each of the Commodore 64 BASIC keywords and functions. A handy reference guide, organized like a dictionary.

THE EASY GUIDE TO YOUR COMMODORE 64™
by Joseph Kascmer
160 pp., illustr., Ref. 0-129
A friendly introduction to using the Commodore 64.

YOUR FIRST VIC-20™ PROGRAM
by Rodnay Zaks
150 pp., illustr., Ref. 0-129
A fully illustrated, easy-to-use introduction to VIC-20 BASIC programming. Will have the reader programming in a matter of hours.

THE VIC-20™ CONNECTION
by James W. Coffron
260 pp., 120 illustr., Ref. 0-128
Teaches elementary interfacing and BASIC programming of the VIC-20 for connection to external devices and household appliances.

YOUR FIRST COMMODORE 64™ PROGRAM
by Rodnay Zaks
182 pp., illustr., Ref. 0-172
You can learn to write simple programs without any prior knowledge of mathematics or computers! Guided by colorful illustrations and step-by-step instructions, you'll be constructing programs within an hour or two.

COMMODORE 64™ BASIC PROGRAMS IN MINUTES
by Stanley R. Trost
170 pp., illustr., Ref. 0-154
Here is a practical set of programs for business, finance, real estate, data analysis, record keeping and educational applications.

GRAPHICS GUIDE TO THE COMMODORE 64™
by Charles Platt
192 pp., illustr., Ref. 0-138
This easy-to-understand book will appeal to anyone who wants to master the Commodore 64's powerful graphics features.

IBM

THE ABC'S OF THE IBM® PC
by Joan Lasselle and Carol Ramsay
100 pp., illustr., Ref. 0-102
This is the book that will take you through the first crucial steps in learning to use the IBM PC.

THE BEST OF IBM® PC SOFTWARE
by Stanley R. Trost
144 pp., illustr., Ref. 0-104
Separates the wheat from the chaff in the world of IBM PC software. Tells you what to expect from the best available IBM PC programs.

THE IBM® PC-DOS HANDBOOK
by Richard Allen King
144 pp., illustr., Ref. 0-103
Explains the PC disk operating system, giving the user better control over the system. Get the most out of your PC by adapting its capabilities to your specific needs.

BUSINESS GRAPHICS FOR THE IBM® PC
by Nelson Ford
200 pp., illustr., Ref. 0-124
Ready-to-run programs for creating line graphs, complex illustrative multiple bar graphs, picture graphs, and more. An ideal way to use your PC's business capabilities!

THE IBM® PC CONNECTION
by James W. Coffron
200 pp., illustr., Ref. 0-127
Teaches elementary interfacing and BASIC programming of the IBM PC for connection to external devices and household appliances.

BASIC EXERCISES FOR THE IBM® PERSONAL COMPUTER
by J.P. Lamoitier
252 pp., 90 illustr., Ref. 0-088
Teaches IBM BASIC through actual practice, using graduated exercises drawn from everyday applications.

USEFUL BASIC PROGRAMS FOR THE IBM® PC
by Stanley R. Trost
144 pp., Ref. 0-111
This collection of programs takes full advantage of the interactive capabilities of your IBM Personal Computer. Financial calculations, investment analysis, record keeping, and math practice—made easier on your IBM PC.

YOUR FIRST IBM® PC PROGRAM
by Rodnay Zaks
182 pp., illustr., Ref. 0-171
This well-illustrated book makes programming easy for children and adults.

YOUR IBM® PC JUNIOR
by Douglas Hergert
250 pp., illustr., Ref. 0-179
This comprehensive reference guide to IBM's most economical microcomputer offers many practical applications and all the helpful information you'll need to get started with your IBM PC Junior.

DATA FILE PROGRAMMING ON YOUR IBM® PC
by Alan Simpson
275 pp., illustr., Ref. 0-146
This book provides instructions and examples of managing data files in BASIC. Programming designs and developments are extensively discussed.

APPLE II® BASIC HANDBOOK
by Douglas Hergert
144 pp., illustr., Ref. 0-155
A complete listing with descriptions and instructive examples of each of the Apple II BASIC keywords and functions. A handy reference guide, organized like a dictionary.

APPLE II® BASIC PROGRAMS IN MINUTES
by Stanley R. Trost
150 pp., illustr., Ref. 0-121
A collection of ready-to-run programs for financial calculations, investment analysis, record keeping, and many more home and office applications. These programs can be entered on your Apple II plus or IIe in minutes!

YOUR FIRST APPLE II® PROGRAM
by Rodnay Zaks
150 pp., illustr., Ref. 0-136
A fully illustrated, easy-to-use introduction to APPLE BASIC programming. Will have the reader programming in a matter of hours.

THE APPLE® CONNECTION
by James W. Coffron
264 pp., 120 illustr., Ref. 0-085
Teaches elementary interfacing and BASIC programming of the Apple for connection to external devices and household appliances.

Apple

THE EASY GUIDE TO YOUR APPLE II®
by Joseph Kascmer
160 pp., illustr., Ref. 0-122
A friendly introduction to using the Apple II, II plus and the new IIe.

BASIC EXERCISES FOR THE APPLE®
by J.P. Lamoitier
250 pp., 90 illustr., Ref. 0-084
Teaches Apple BASIC through actual practice, using graduated exercises drawn from everyday applications.

TRS-80

YOUR COLOR COMPUTER
by Doug Mosher
350 pp., illustr., Ref. 0-097
Patience and humor guide the reader through purchasing, setting up, programming, and using the Radio Shack TRS-80/TDP Series 100 Color Computer. A complete introduction.

THE FOOLPROOF GUIDE TO SCRIPSIT™ WORD PROCESSING
by Jeff Berner

225 pp., illustr., Ref. 0-098
Everything you need to know about SCRIPSIT—from starting out, to mastering document editing. This user-friendly guide is written in plain English, with a touch of wit.

Timex/Sinclair 1000/ZX81

YOUR TIMEX/SINCLAIR 1000 AND ZX81™
by Douglas Hergert
159 pp., illustr., Ref. 0-099
This book explains the set-up, operation, and capabilities of the Timex/Sinclair 1000 and ZX81. Includes how to interface peripheral devices, and introduces BASIC programming.

THE TIMEX/SINCLAIR 1000™ BASIC HANDBOOK
by Douglas Hergert
170 pp., illustr., Ref. 0-113
A complete alphabetical listing with explanations and examples of each word in the T/S 1000 BASIC vocabulary; will allow you quick, error-free programming of your T/S 1000.

TIMEX/SINCLAIR 1000™ BASIC PROGRAMS IN MINUTES
by Stanley R. Trost
150 pp., illustr., Ref. 0-119
A collection of ready-to-run programs for financial calculations, investment analysis, record keeping, and many more home and office applications. These programs can be entered on your T/S 1000 in minutes!

MORE USES FOR YOUR TIMEX/SINCLAIR 1000™
Astronomy on Your Computer
by Eric Burgess
176 pp., illustr., Ref. 0-112
Ready-to-run programs that turn your TV into a planetarium.

Other Popular Computers

YOUR FIRST TI 99/4A™ PROGRAM
by Rodnay Zaks

182 pp., illustr., Ref. 0-157
Colorfully illustrated, this book concentrates on the essentials of programming in a clear, entertaining fashion.

THE RADIO SHACK® NOTEBOOK COMPUTER
by Orson Kellogg
128 pp., illustr., Ref. 0-150
Whether you already have the Radio Shack Model 100 notebook computer, or are interested in buying one, this book will clearly explain what it can do for you.

THE EASY GUIDE TO YOUR COLECO ADAM™
by Thomas Blackadar
175 pp., illustr., Ref. 0-181
This quick reference guide shows you how to get started on your Coleco Adam with a minimum of technical jargon.

YOUR KAYPRO II/4/10™
by Andrea Reid and Gary Deidrichs
250 pp., illustr., Ref. 0-166
This book is a non-technical introduction to the KAYPRO family of computers. You will find all you need to know about operating your KAYPRO within this one complete guide.

Software and Applications

Operating Systems

THE CP/M® HANDBOOK
by Rodnay Zaks
320 pp., 100 illustr., Ref 0-048
An indispensable reference and guide to CP/M—the most widely-used operating system for small computers.

MASTERING CP/M®
by Alan R. Miller
398 pp., illustr., Ref. 0-068
For advanced CP/M users or systems programmers who want maximum use of the CP/M operating system . . . takes up where our *CP/M Handbook* leaves off.

THE BEST OF
CP/M® SOFTWARE
by John D. Halamka
250 pp., illustr., Ref. 0-100
This book reviews tried-and-tested, commercially available software for your CP/M system.

REAL WORLD UNIX™
by John D. Halamka
250 pp., illustr., Ref. 0-093
This book is written for the beginning and intermediate UNIX user in a practical, straightforward manner, with specific instructions given for many special applications.

THE CP/M PLUS™ HANDBOOK
by Alan R. Miller
250 pp., illustr., Ref. 0-158
This guide is easy for the beginner to understand, yet contains valuable information for advanced users of CP/M Plus (Version 3).

Business Software

INTRODUCTION TO
WORDSTAR™
by Arthur Naiman
202 pp., 30 illustr., Ref. 0-077
Makes it easy to learn how to use WordStar, a powerful word processing program for personal computers.

PRACTICAL WORDSTAR™ USES
by Julie Anne Arca
200 pp., illustr., Ref. 0-107
Pick your most time-consuming office tasks and this book will show you how to streamline them with WordStar.

MASTERING VISICALC®
by Douglas Hergert
217 pp., 140 illustr., Ref. 0-090
Explains how to use the VisiCalc "electronic spreadsheet" functions and provides examples of each. Makes using this powerful program simple.

DOING BUSINESS WITH
VISICALC®
by Stanley R. Trost
260 pp., Ref. 0-086
Presents accounting and management

planning applications—from financial statements to master budgets; from pricing models to investment strategies.

DOING BUSINESS WITH
SUPERCALC™
by Stanley R. Trost
248 pp., illustr., Ref. 0-095
Presents accounting and management planning applications—from financial statements to master budgets; from pricing models to investment strategies.

VISICALC® FOR SCIENCE AND
ENGINEERING
by Stanley R. Trost and
Charles Pomernacki
225 pp., illustr., Ref. 0-096
More than 50 programs for solving technical problems in the science and engineering fields. Applications range from math and statistics to electrical and electronic engineering.

DOING BUSINESS WITH 1-2-3™
by Stanley R. Trost
250 pp., illustr., Ref. 0-159
If you are a business professional using the 1-2-3 software package, you will find the spreadsheet and graphics models provided in this book easy to use "as is" in everyday business situations.

THE ABC'S OF 1-2-3™
by Chris Gilbert
225 pp., illustr., Ref. 0-168
For those new to the LOTUS 1-2-3 program, this book offers step-by-step instructions in mastering its spreadsheet, data base, and graphing capabilities.

UNDERSTANDING dBASE II™
by Alan Simpson
220 pp., illustr., Ref. 0-147
Learn programming techniques for mailing label systems, bookkeeping and data base management, as well as ways to interface dBASE II with other software systems.

DOING BUSINESS WITH
dBASE II™
by Stanley R. Trost
250 pp., illustr., Ref. 0-160
Learn to use dBASE II for accounts receivable, recording business income

and expenses, keeping personal records and mailing lists, and much more.

DOING BUSINESS WITH MULTIPLAN™
by Richard Allen King and Stanley R. Trost
250 pp., illustr., Ref. 0-148
This book will show you how using Multiplan can be nearly as easy as learning to use a pocket calculator. It presents a collection of templates that can be applied "as is" to business situations.

DOING BUSINESS WITH PFS®
by Stanley R. Trost
250 pp., illustr., Ref. 0-161
This practical guide describes specific business and personal applications in detail. Learn to use PFS for accounting, data analysis, mailing lists and more.

INFOPOWER: PRACTICAL INFOSTAR™ USES
by Jule Anne Arca and Charles F. Pirro
275 pp., illustr., Ref. 0-108
This book gives you an overview of InfoStar, including DataStar and ReportStar, WordStar, MailMerge, and SuperSort. Hands on exercises take you step-by-step through real life business applications.

WRITING WITH EASYWRITER II™
by Douglas W. Topham
250 pp., illustr., Ref. 0-141
Friendly style, handy illustrations, and numerous sample exercises make it easy to learn the EasyWriter II word processing system.

Business Applications

INTRODUCTION TO WORD PROCESSING
by Hal Glatzer
205 pp., 140 illustr., Ref. 0-076
Explains in plain language what a word processor can do, how it improves productivity, how to use a word processor and how to buy one wisely.

COMPUTER POWER FOR YOUR LAW OFFICE
by Daniel Remer
225 pp., Ref. 0-109

How to use computers to reach peak productivity in your law office, simply and inexpensively.

OFFICE EFFICIENCY WITH PERSONAL COMPUTERS
by Sheldon Crop
175 pp., illustr., Ref. 0-165
Planning for computerization of your office? This book provides a simplified discussion of the challenges involved for everyone from business owner to clerical worker.

COMPUTER POWER FOR YOUR ACCOUNTING OFFICE
by James Morgan
250 pp., illustr., Ref. 0-164
This book is a convenient source of information about computerizing you accounting office, with an emphasis on hardware and software options.

Languages

C

UNDERSTANDING C
by Bruce Hunter
200 pp., Ref 0-123
Explains how to use the powerful C language for a variety of applications. Some programming experience assumed.

FIFTY C PROGRAMS
by Bruce Hunter
200 pp., illustr., Ref. 0-155
Beginning as well as intermediate C programmers will find this a useful guide to programming techniques and specific applications.

BUSINESS PROGRAMS IN C
by Leon Wortman and Thomas O. Sidebottom
200 pp., illustr., Ref. 0-153
This book provides source code listings of C programs for the business person or experienced programmer. Each easy-to-follow tutorial applies directly to a business situation.

BASIC

YOUR FIRST BASIC PROGRAM
by Rodnay Zaks
150pp. illustr. in color, Ref. 0-129
A "how-to-program" book for the first time computer user, aged 8 to 88.

FIFTY BASIC EXERCISES
by J. P. Lamoitier
232 pp., 90 illustr., Ref. 0-056
Teaches BASIC by actual practice, using graduated exercises drawn from everyday applications. All programs written in Microsoft BASIC.

INSIDE BASIC GAMES
by Richard Mateosian
348 pp., 120 illustr., Ref. 0-055
Teaches interactive BASIC programming through games. Games are written in Microsoft BASIC and can run on the TRS-80, Apple II and PET/CBM.

BASIC FOR BUSINESS
by Douglas Hergert
224 pp., 15 illustr., Ref. 0-080
A logically organized, no-nonsense introduction to BASIC programming for business applications. Includes many fully-explained accounting programs, and shows you how to write them.

EXECUTIVE PLANNING WITH BASIC
by X. T. Bui
196 pp., 19 illustr., Ref. 0-083
An important collection of business management decision models in BASIC, including Inventory Management (EOQ), Critical Path Analysis and PERT, Financial Ratio Analysis, Portfolio Management, and much more.

BASIC PROGRAMS FOR SCIENTISTS AND ENGINEERS
by Alan R. Miller
318 pp., 120 illustr., Ref. 0-073
This book from the "Programs for Scientists and Engineers" series provides a library of problem-solving programs while developing proficiency in BASIC.

CELESTIAL BASIC
by Eric Burgess
300 pp., 65 illustr., Ref. 0-087
A collection of BASIC programs that rapidly complete the chores of typical astronomical computations. It's like having a planetarium in your own home! Displays apparent movement of stars, planets and meteor showers.

YOUR SECOND BASIC PROGRAM
by Gary Lippman
250 pp., illustr., Ref. 0-152
A sequel to *Your First BASIC Program*, this book follows the same patient, detailed approach and brings you to the next level of programming skill.

Pascal

INTRODUCTION TO PASCAL (Including UCSD Pascal™)
by Rodnay Zaks
420 pp., 130 illustr., Ref. 0-066
A step-by-step introduction for anyone wanting to learn the Pascal language. Describes UCSD and Standard Pascals. No technical background is assumed.

THE PASCAL HANDBOOK
by Jacques Tiberghien
486 pp., 270 illustr., Ref. 0-053
A dictionary of the Pascal language, defining every reserved word, operator, procedure and function found in all major versions of Pascal.

APPLE® PASCAL GAMES
by Douglas Hergert and Joseph T. Kalash
372 pp., 40 illustr., Ref. 0-074
A collection of the most popular computer games in Pascal, challenging the reader not only to play but to investigate how games are implemented on the computer.

INTRODUCTION TO THE UCSD p-SYSTEM™
by Charles W. Grant and Jon Butah
300 pp., 10 illustr., Ref. 0-061

A simple, clear introduction to the UCSD Pascal Operating System; for beginners through experienced programmers.

PASCAL PROGRAMS FOR SCIENTISTS AND ENGINEERS
by Alan R. Miller
374 pp., 120 illustr., Ref. 0-058
A comprehensive collection of frequently used algorithms for scientific and technical applications, programmed in Pascal. Includes such programs as curve-fitting, integrals and statistical techniques.

DOING BUSINESS WITH PASCAL
by Richard Hergert and Douglas Hergert
371 pp., illustr., Ref. 0-091
Practical tips for using Pascal in business programming. Includes design considerations, language extensions, and applications examples.

Assembly Language Programming

PROGRAMMING THE 6502
by Rodnay Zaks
386 pp., 160 illustr., Ref. 0-046
Assembly language programming for the 6502, from basic concepts to advanced data structures.

6502 APPLICATIONS
by Rodnay Zaks
278 pp., 200 illustr., Ref. 0-015
Real-life application techniques: the input/output book for the 6502.

ADVANCED 6502 PROGRAMMING
by Rodnay Zaks
292 pp., 140 illustr., Ref. 0-089
Third in the 6502 series. Teaches more advanced programming techniques, using games as a framework for learning.

PROGRAMMING THE Z80
by Rodnay Zaks
624 pp., 200 illustr., Ref. 0-069
A complete course in programming the Z80 microprocessor and a thorough introduction to assembly language.

Z80 APPLICATIONS
by James W. Coffron
288 pp., illustr., Ref. 0-094
Covers techniques and applications for using peripheral devices with a Z80 based system.

PROGRAMMING THE 6809
by Rodnay Zaks and William Labiak
362 pp., 150 illustr., Ref. 0-078
This book explains how to program the 6809 in assembly language. No prior programming knowledge required.

PROGRAMMING THE Z8000
by Richard Mateosian
298 pp., 124 illustr., Ref. 0-032
How to program the Z8000 16-bit microprocessor. Includes a description of the architecture and function of the Z8000 and its family of support chips.

PROGRAMMING THE 8086/8088
by James W. Coffron
300 pp., illustr., Ref. 0-120
This book explains how to program the 8086 and 8088 in assembly language. No prior programming knowledge required.

Other Languages

FORTRAN PROGRAMS FOR SCIENTISTS AND ENGINEERS
by Alan R. Miller
280 pp., 120 illustr., Ref. 0-082
In the "Programs for Scientists and Engineers" series, this book provides specific scientific and engineering application programs written in FORTRAN.

A MICROPROGRAMMED APL IMPLEMENTATION
by Rodnay Zaks
350 pp., Ref. 0-005
An expert-level text presenting the complete conceptual analysis and design of an APL interpreter, and actual listing of the microcode.

SYBEX COMPUTER BOOKS

are different.

Here is why . . .

At SYBEX, each book is designed with you in mind. Every manuscript is carefully selected and supervised by our editors, who are themselves computer experts. We publish the best authors, whose technical expertise is matched by an ability to write clearly and to communicate effectively. Programs are thoroughly tested for accuracy by our technical staff. Our computerized production department goes to great lengths to make sure that each book is well-designed.

In the pursuit of timeliness, SYBEX has achieved many publishing firsts. SYBEX was among the first to integrate personal computers used by authors and staff into the publishing process. SYBEX was the first to publish books on the CP/M operating system, microprocessor interfacing techniques, word processing, and many more topics.

Expertise in computers and dedication to the highest quality product have made SYBEX a world leader in computer book publishing. Translated into fourteen languages, SYBEX books have helped millions of people around the world to get the most from their computers. We hope we have helped you, too.

For a complete catalog of our publications please contact:

U.S.A.	FRANCE	GERMANY
SYBEX, Inc.	SYBEX	SYBEX-Verlag GmbH
2344 Sixth Street	6–8 Impasse du Curé	Vogelsanger Weg 111
Berkeley,	75018 Paris	4000 Düsseldorf 30
California 94710	France	West Germany
Tel: (800) 227-2346	Tel: 01/203–9595	Tel: (0211) 626411
(415) 848-8233	Telex: 211801	Telex: 8588163
Telex: 336311		